THE HOOD ENTREPRENEUR

THE HOOD ENTREPRENEUR

Sephuine Morgan

Published by JLG Publishing
www.jlgpublishing.weebly.com

THE HOOD ENTREPRENEUR

ISBN 978-0-995-66411-1

Book formatted by www.bookformatting.co.uk.

Contents

Acknowledgements

First and foremost, I would like to thank the universe for granting me with my wish. I have been battling with my desire to write, for just over 10 years and I have finally completed the first step on my journey. As a teenager I would write poems, keep journals and even write numerous letters to my best friends. I am so happy to be sharing my talent with you. Thank you

I would like to express my deepest appreciation to my dear friend and mentor Jenica Leah, who has never given up on me despite the tribulations we have faced on this path. You shared my vision and helped me to bring it to life with your knowledge and consistency. When I felt like throwing the towel in, you reassured me with wisdom and filled me with positivity. Thank You for believing in me.

An extended thank you goes out to my dear mother Valerie Martin. I commend your strengths and efforts that you have consistently shown throughout my life. So brave, so fearless and so strong. I would not be who I am today without your guidance. Thank you for always showing me support and being on the other end of the phone to just say hi. I love you mom.

I have to show sincere gratitude to Craig Pinkney. I appreciate what you have done for me, I expressed my need for your input when we sat down for a coffee meeting at the university and I knew that it would have paid off. Thank you so much for your time, with so much on your schedule you still managed to deliver the best.

Finally, I want to say a massive thank you to, Jermaine Alleyne, Tanisha Blake, Cherelle Martin, Chantel Sachanna, Cynthia Blake, Birdel Benjamin, Halicia Ward, Wayne McFarquar, Natalie Blake, Adam Brux and Deeno designs, for all the work that you have inputted on this journey. I appreciate you all, without you guys, it wouldn't have been possible. Thank you.

Foreword

There are a few times when a writer is able to encapsulate the essence of the human journey from the struggle to success. For youth within Great Britain, often times, there are so many distractions from the likes of social media, negative environments, lack of opportunities, miss-education and the lack of support they need to navigate through life.

Growing up in a similar environment to Sephuine, I believe it is imperative that those whom are like minded stick together, support and assist each other in their endeavours. Why? Because, we live in environments where jealousy, hatred and negative self-concepts are internalised as norms which often creates a barrier for people to grow.

Sephuine Morgan's self-help book, is an inspiring and motivational contribution to the forward thinkers. Those that read the book should expect to be challenged to learn, gather ideas and create a new dimension within your mind to realise that, no matter where you come from, no matter your circumstances, you can break free and break the cycle.

There is an African proverb that states that 'each one, should teach one' and this book cannot be under estimated as a critical contribution to the mental liberation of all people and not just the youth going through the 'struggle', seeking success.

I am proud to see another light shine within my community, which will be another building block for those who may be looking for guidance and knowledge to overcome adversity.

Craig Pinkney

Welcome

Welcome to the reading of The Hood Entrepreneur. This book is based on a true account of my life story and will take you on a journey of mastery. The book will explore how I changed from a snotty teenager raised in the ghetto, to an aspiring young adult.

After procrastinating for 10 years, I have decided to share my story which was birthed by a shift in my mindset. I knew that this would help millions of people across the world and I just became desperate to get my message out. If you follow the key principles in this book, you will be influenced to start your own business, explore your career options and educate yourself financially, using the skills and talents that you already have within you.

With the economic climate decreasing every day, you are no longer safe in a job. I am here to revitalise all the golden nuggets you have within and to get you starting something that serves you well and makes you money. Everyone has to start somewhere and you have chosen to start with this book. Thank you.

Having dreams and goals is achievable by anyone—and I mean anyone—you have dream's, don't you? We all dream but what separates the winners from the losers is the action taken to achieve your dreams. I want you to really take that in and digest it. Action is everything. You have to physically move and the time is now! I am hoping that by the end of this book, you will understand, anything is possible as long as you can see it in your head for yourself.

If you complete all of the challenges set out for you; be consistent with them, being totally HONEST with yourself, then I can assure you, this book will change your life.

Just to give you an understanding of where I am coming from, the area which I grew up in was made up with a very small percentage of smart working folk (people that were paid a lot for doing a little) mixed with a larger percentage of hard working folk (people that were overworked and underpaid). Most people were poor and had been taught using the principles of a poor man's mindset. The term 'poor man's mindset', simply defines someone who is financially uneducated.

Most people were uneducated in my area with little or no one in the family attending university. It was clear which families had money and which did not from the things you owned. Mine was one of the families that never had much, although my mom did a pretty good job at making us believe otherwise. We never owned anything!

I come from a place where all opportunities appear difficult to reach and not much people believe in themselves or even believe they are going to make it out of the hood. I grew up with the same mentality. This was life for me and as a little girl, I struggled to imagine what things would be like on the 'rich side' of life.

I was surrounded by gang culture, knife and gun crime. There was always some drama going on, from fights to actual murders and I express some of those stories within this book in order for you to grasp the context of where I started, to where I am now. Which I know that so many of you can relate.

Throughout the book, I want you to read, learn, apply and keep on doing that over and over again. When you have done that, find the motivational section in the book that resonates with you in accordance to whatever you are going through in life and highlight the bits that mean the most. I then challenge you to find a solution using the methods presented in the book, until you feel certain enough to challenge that area within your life. What you will find is that, depending on what you are experiencing in life, whether it be career wise, financial struggles, family, relationships or finding yourself; different things will stick out to you that you hadn't noticed when first reading it. Most of the books that have taught me great wisdom and have been relevant to my life, I have read over ten times.

I strongly recommended that you complete all the tasks given in the book, they will ensure that your daily habits become good, positive things that can help better your life.

I want you to use my situations, compare them to your own and find a way to turn negatives into positives. It is important that you always look on the bright side of life because this type of mindset can change your future.

Although it was tough for me, I had to train my mind to do things every day that kept me away from a life that I didn't want. I had to seek out professional people whom I viewed as role models and find out what they were doing in order to obtain what they have. And I never stop doing this, because there is always room for improvement. Investing in yourself is one of life's best values. But you have to start with believing in yourself. There is no better way to build yourself up, than by telling yourself how great and worthy you are...Literally! You may, or may not have heard the notion of positive affirmations before. Well, when I first heard about them I thought, what absolute madness! But that was because my mind was in a different place and I wasn't willing to change my attitude even though I wanted change.

After my ignorance and disbelief about positive affirmations, I gave them a go anyway because eventually, I was open to changing my life. I wanted better and I knew I had to change whatever I was doing to ensure I had better.

Task 1

Now to get you started, I have a short exercise that I want you to practice—make sure you are alone, take the book to a mirror—come on get up and find a mirror in your home, or in your pocket... seriously. If you cannot find one then I need you to take your camera phone out and go to camera, put it in selfie mode so that you are staring at your own reflection. Once you can see yourself I want you to say "Who am I". Say this out loud and then follow that by saying "I AM".

Then I want you to voice the first thing that comes to your mind after the words 'I AM'.

Some examples may be;

- I AM Amazing
- I AM Love
- I AM Rich
- I AM A Good Mother/ Father
- I AM Beautiful
- I AM Healthy
- I AM Courageous
- I AM Unique
- I AM Enough
- I AM A Billionaire

Whatever you said after the words 'I AM' is a representation of how you describe yourself at this current moment. However, the end of the sentence will always be different and relative to your current experiences. Do not be disconcert if the words are not great, amazing positive words. This task is about honesty and you have to be honest with yourself in order to experience growth and change.

I know you may question if two words can change your life and it may all seem a little farfetched if you have not reconciled with these words previously. However, the words 'I AM' have the power to change your life; just trust that what I am telling you is the truth.

By saying these words, you are confirming to your sub-conscious beliefs and to the universe, that you are what you say you are and eventually you will become what you believe. This phrase is powerful enough to instruct the body with things to do, according to what you say after the words 'I AM'. This is why we have to be mindful of the thoughts that we are paying attention to and the things that we are saying about ourselves because only you can decide who you are and who you are going to be.

Feel free to use the words above as examples. You may have completed the task above using negative phrases to describe yourself, the process however, is still the same. You will become exactly what you think and tell yourself that you are.

You may feel a slight sense of discomfort completing that task for the first few times. However, you have to step out of your comfort zone and do things that you don't necessarily like doing, in order to obtain a different end result.

If you did not do that exercise then I hope you try it at some point whilst reading this book. I will later show you how using that exercise changed my life. I hope you enjoy the read, sit back, be open minded, judge if you please and take something positive from this experience.

Welcome to 'The Hood Entrepreneur'.

Chapter 1:
Hood Life

Fifty-five thousand pounds a year! Yep that's what I'm going to be, an independent reviewing officer. This job is going to be amazing and I'm going to be rich. I can finally get that Porsche I always wanted. So by calculation, by the time I get to the age of 25, I will have my own yard (home), my sexy Porsche and cash in my bank. This will shut my dad up... and my mom actually, I need to go and tell her. Mom and Dad are always flipping nagging me to do good with my life. Just let me breathe, I get it!

(Meet Seph: An ambitious young girl who comes from a large family that have grown up in Winson Green, also known as the hood. The hood aka neighbourhood: A place where opportunities appear unsurfaced and people only dream of making it out).

"Mom! Mommmmmmmm!" Flipping hell, I'm going to have to go downstairs to her, seems as though she's acting as if she cannot hear me. Maybe me stamping down every step will get her attention. RUDE! Why do parents do that? My mom shouts my name when I'm upstairs to come all the way downstairs to get the remote that's right next to her and if it's not the remote it's a drink from the fridge in the kitchen that's approximately seven and a half steps away – if you're a shoe size 7. Bloody lazy I tell you. But when I call her, she's acting as if she cannot hear me. I do not think that's fair!

"Mom," I shouted. Near her ear hole just to make sure she could hear me this time. "I am gassed (excited), you know how you and my dad keep going on about me going to college and University

7

and getting a good education blah blah blah? Well, I have figured it all out Mom. I've got a plan, nothing outrageous or illegal this time, a serious plan to get us out of this area for good like you always wanted." I sat down to explain the thoughts going through my head.

(Meet Mom: Single mother with six children. Works three jobs to support them but is paid peanuts, so the family is quite poor financially but rich with love. Mom is very loving and would do anything to ensure that her children are happy).

Mom had her feet rested up on the puffet and did not seem like she believed my plan was serious this time. She kept her head to the TV flicking through all the channels with the remote.

"Urgh, come on then, tell me what it is now." she said. Acting like she was bothered about my masterplan that took me time to think up.

"Well I have decided that I want to be an Independent reviewing officer."

"A What." she said. Having no idea what I was talking about.

"An I.R.O." I broke it down for her as if it would have made it easier to understand.

"What the hell is that?" she moaned,

"Well basically, I will be the chairman, well chairwoman in some really important meetings of children living in children's homes and I will have to decide what happens with many of these young people's lives. Top of the social work ladder mom to cut a long story short. It's a big deal! I will make a lot of money if I do this, then I will buy you a house, me a house, I will get ma Porsche and then me, you and your army of children will be nice – set for life. How does that sound?" I laughed as I walked around the room trying to block the tv so that she would give me all of her attention.

"Sounds great Seph." My mom sounded more like she could get down with this idea, opposed to the one I came to her with last week that suggested we rob a bank—set it off style—like the 1996 American crime action film. Of course, I was Queen Latifah in that scenario. I think my mom actually noted that down as a serious career idea.

"You're always full of ideas, just like your dad. Seph you're going to be good at anything you do, you have the drive and the passion, you have always been like that since you were a baby, cheeky and determined." Mom giggled whilst she reminisced, I could tell she was picturing my cute little face for a minute until the stare she was doing became extensive.

"You do know that I can't afford to pay for you to do no college or University course though?" She uttered. "I will have to work as much as I can to see what I can contribute but I can't make any promises." Mom was always so supportive of what I wanted to do and just wanted the best for all of her children. I could see that she felt helpless but I was about to put that feeling to an end.

"Na mom, things have changed. There are lots of opportunities for us young people nowadays, we just have to work super hard or know someone that knows someone. College is free Mom and for University, I can get a loan or some funding that pays for my course, then I pay it back when I secure my job. Trust me, I will do all my research and work as hard as I can, we are going to be nice. I got us. You and your army of kids." I exclaimed.

5: 30pm! Shit, is that the time, I've got to go and get ready.

"Mom I'm off. Going to my dad's now, he's outside. I will be back on Sunday at the usual time." I shouted to mum, as I raced upstairs to pack my stuff and meet my Dad who was never late to collect me. Rushing around in a manic, I began dragging things from my chest of drawers whilst knocking everything on top of it down. I wasn't about to stop to tidy it up, I didn't want my dad to start moaning about me getting in the car two minutes after 5: 30pm. After packing my bag messily, I was ready to go.

"Love you." I muttered to Mom, barely loud enough for a mouse to hear. Come on, you know I couldn't say it too loud because I was a cool kid. Saying 'I love you' would have emphasised my emotional side and made me look like a wimp and I sure wasn't a wimp. I know what you're thinking, it's your mom; the most important person ever who you should love the most, I should be able to just say it. Well I'm too gangster to say that shit out loud and you're going to know the gangster me later... Joke!

Anyway, getting back on track, I never told my mom that I

loved her out loud because it just felt uncomfortable. I mean, she must know I love her though, she can feel it.

"Later you lot, I'm off to my dad's." I shouted to my siblings. The term 'my dad' used because I had a different father to my siblings. This was common in Winson Green, single moms with children that had different fathers. I mean, the different fathers bit was less common but if you weren't a single mom, you were not popping (cool) since it was the norm to be a single mom. If you lived with your dad you may have been considered posh, lucky, or even royal.

I loved having my own dad and I loved my dad very much. I was definitely a daddy's girl growing up—a gangster one—or so I liked to believe! You see growing up in Winson Green, you learnt from your elders that you had to be strong and never really show an emotional side to you or else you would be teased. You had to show that you could stick up for yourself. So, I took that literally and built a whole new alter ego who was a gangster chick that couldn't be messed with, or else she'd get really ugly and beat someone up. Or even kill them as she used to say a lot. Thank God that alter ego lived in me and no one tested the waters as I don't know what I would have done.

Going to my dad's was like a luxury weekend away. Dad lived in the same area as the enemies or 'ops' as people in my area called them, he lived in Aston. Luckily for dad I was a girl and did not have to worry too much about the whole postcode mafia war in Birmingham. I was however, considered dodgy by some of the kids in Aston when I told them where I was from, some even nicknamed me Con-Girl. I quite liked the sound of the name actually but hated what it stood for. I didn't care about the postcode war, I was just happy to be friends with anyone I met.

I always got everything that I wanted when I went with Dad. From the minute I got in the car, it was like living the rich life. My dad drove a brand-new gold Rover 75. It had heated leather seats, electric windows, mini TV screens in the head rests of the seats and he always had the best movies playing. The Lion King was one of my favourites.

Food was unlimited at Dad's with it being just him and me most of the time. I was always sure to get £20 pocket money and a trip to town to go shopping because I always needed something. Mom would always say, when I asked her for things, "Tell your dad to buy it, I feed, clothe and keep a roof over your head every day." So that's exactly what I done. I always made out like I needed something so that every weekend would be a shopping trip. That's how I always ended up with the latest trainers.

My dad lived a rich and happy life and seemed to have no problems. He wouldn't moan when I asked for things so I never had a problem asking. It never made sense in the real world; him and Mom being separated. They were both such amazing people, very attractive and just a perfect match. I never dared ask my mom why they split up, I mentioned it a few times to my dad and he always replied with "When you're older Seph I will tell you everything. I love your mom and I always will."

I was spoilt rotten by Dad, being his only daughter. I had two bedrooms in his three-story house. One room was for when my sisters or cousins would come over. It was a large freshly painted room, very clean and had three bunk beds in there. All the beds had quilts and pillows in the packets just waiting for my guests to come over, even the mattresses were still covered in plastic. I never got a chance to make my friends stay over at that house as Dad had moved before then.

My other room was huge, it had a double bed with my favourite coloured purple sheets and was filled with lots of pillows and fluffy cushions. I had a soft black rug at the end of my bed that covered most of the marble heated flooring. Some of my favourite Damage posters were stuck on the wall and looked amazing when my spotlights were on, as it gave the effect of a concert. My room was the type of room you would see on MTV cribs. It was just great!

As beautiful as both rooms were, I never slept in none of the rooms as much as I slept in Dad's. His room had a super king-sized bed with an electric blanket that was always on, soft sheets that smelt like fresh washing and was loaded with 500ml bottles of Volvic water. I later began to realise that the heated blanket and water was there because my dad was battling with his sickle cell; a disease which affected his red blood cells. I just knew that keeping warm was a priority for him, so bedtimes were always cosy.

When I slept in Dad's room, it was like being in a hotel with maids. As much as I made a mess he would always scurry around, cleaning up after me, doing such a great job that I wouldn't notice the mess I made. I would get lost in the sheets with my bedtime snacks and water whilst watching a DVD on the 55 inch TV that had surround speakers. My dad would be sat at one of many computers doing whatever the hell he was doing.

(Meet Dad: A Denzel Washington lookalike who had it all – he was a technology geek and knew how to build computers from scratch. He worked for himself and used to secure amazing work contracts with companies that would pay him huge amounts of money. He also had a side hustle, where he would sell DVDS and CDs that he had copied off from the computer).

"Seph, shall we go to the cinemas tomorrow or do you want to go to town to buy something?" Dad asked.

"Dad, can we go to auntie's house, I want to see my cousins, I haven't seen them for ages." I said.

"Seph you were with them last weekend when I had you."

"Yeh but I want to see them again, please Dad." I pleaded in hope that he would say yes straight away. We hadn't arrived at Dad's house yet, so I was hoping he would have diverted and went straight to my aunties.

I gave my dad the look, the look that I mastered at the age of five or maybe even before that. The 'how can you say no to your princess look'. "DAAAAAD!" I moaned. I didn't even have to wait for a reply for that. It was a yes and just like that we went off to my cousins' house.

Now I grew up calling my neighbourhood "The hood, the ends, the zones, the bits, the block." It had all types of names but my cousins lived in an area deemed as more dangerous than mine, the ghetto also known as Newtown!

This was some real-life gangster shit. You would see people sitting on the walls drinking their drinks and smoking their weed, music was playing loud either from multiple cars or from a large speaker and everyone would be on the block chilling. The area was covered in high rise flats with off licenses on every corner, takeaways and parks with no apparatus.

Although this was the ghetto where any average middle class posh person would feel afraid, this was home to us. Summer was always the best at aunties house. Auntie Carol had seven children and those cousins were the best, especially Mya and Jade. They would never make me feel anything less than their sister, I was always told I looked like them which made the whole sister thing a whole lot cooler and believable. I created some of the best memories with my cousins. Good and bad!

I'll share with you something that I would never forget; brace yourself people and let your imagination run wild.

Now I'm guessing you all remember cassette tapes, right? If you said yes then I know you're an 80s/ pre-80s baby, maybe 1991 at the very latest but if you said no then give yourself a clap for being young and fab. Now if you thought music tapes were a throwback, I'm guessing you remember a boyband called Damage. (Four British guys who sung RnB songs; Corey being the sexy one). Well I loved them so much and what typically happened in my neighbourhood was, if you couldn't afford something that you wanted really badly, you just take it… Without paying. Five finger discounts was what some of us called it.

I don't actually know where I learnt that trait. I just know that I went on a spree of theft that ensured I wasn't left out, especially at school when people had things that I knew I couldn't afford. It was a horrible feeling and the only thing that would make it surpass was if I had what everyone else had, even if that meant stealing it from the shops.

Carrying on with my story, my amazing cousin Jade took me to Birmingham city centre. We got off the bus near the ramp (Pallasades) to go to McDonalds before she brought me into a shop called Virgin records. When we got to Virgin, there on the shelf was the Damage album tape saying "Buy me Seph." I think at the time the tape costed around £9.99 and that was too much money to spend on an album that was a tape and not even a CD. With the temptation in me being at the highest point it could have possibly reached, I took the tape off the shelf as an average shopper would. I knew within me that I had no money, I didn't leave my house with any money and I was already due a shopping trip with my dad so he hadn't given me any money.

I glanced around the shop, saw my cousin Jade looking around at all the other CDs and tapes and I can remember quite clearly seeing a geeky looking young male that worked there, stacking a shelf. He never even realised I was there, he looked like the 'trainee of the month' type of guy that was so into his job. He paid me no mind, which was great. With one final glance around the store, I took the chance and put the tape in my pocket. The thrill going through my body at the time was amazing, my heart was beating faster than it ever had before, my fingers were numbing so badly that I couldn't even feel my hands. The sweat dripping off me was enough to fill a bucket and my adrenaline was showing through my fast shaking body and bobbling head. I moved slowly over to where Jade was and on my way, I passed a mirror, realising that none of my described side-affects mentioned above were actually visible. I was not sweaty, nor shaking, I looked fine. "You got this." I proclaimed to myself. I wasn't about to mention a word to my cousin.

I had planned to tell her when I left the shop because I knew how gangster I would have looked and how much ratings I would have got. Jade loved Damage even more than me so this was a win, win situation. A couple of minutes later, I see Jade getting ready to leave the shop. This was perfect timing; a huge smile came on my face as we were heading towards the door. At that point, I knew that in approximately 45 minutes we would be back on the block listening to Damage, and that would have been all down to me. "Seph!" I hear Jade shout me, showing me a poster that was displayed in the window and pointing in the direction of the poster. I started to regret that I never told her I pocketed the tape, maybe she would hurry up. Instead, she carried on browsing. "For flip sake" – the voice in my head shouted as I tried figuring out what my next best move would be. Jade pulled me back to see the poster that she had already pointed out to me. "We have to go cuz." I said anxiously, "My dad is going to wonder where we are."

I told my dad that I was going to Burberry Park, that was just down the road from my aunt's house. "Ok true." She said, as she agreed and we were on our way out. That feeling came again but this time I was more anxious, "It must be showing." I kept talking to myself, looking around hoping that no one clocked on to my thief fetish tape robbery. So close to the door—in my head dancing in a large field with no socks on to my favourite Damage tune— when suddenly I was dragged back to reality. Literally!

"Excuse me! Can you wait here?" The security guard, who I failed to notice when I done my full shop scan, grabbed my arm.

"What the hell are you doing you prick, get off her!" Jade shouted, thinking I was being wrongfully targeted. My older cousins always had my back, especially Mya and Jade. And with Mya not being here, Jade was not about to let the security guard hurt me. At that point, I decided I would go along with my cousin; things were about to get messy.

"Yeah, get the hell off me! Don't touch me you idiot!" I shouted, aggressively, pulling my arm back enough for the security guard to let go. I began acting as I knew best — rowdy and ghetto! I could feel the tape moving around in my pocket each time the security guard tried to hold on to me. I couldn't go down without a fight.

It was so weird because as much as I was acting hard, the disappointment that grew within me stemmed from the collage of images circulating in my head. I could just imagine how this would have made my parents feel and I knew they would have been disappointed in me. After going back and forth with security about them wrongfully accusing me, everything became a blur. The feeling of my parents being upset made me feel shit – I had no more fight left me. I took the tape out of my pocket and was ashamed to look at my cousin that had just wasted so much energy trying to help me. Jade looked at me with disappointment, she never spoke a word. She was shocked and ashamed! I knew instantly that I had embarrassed her. The store manager, the geeky store assistant and the security guard took us to the back of the shop and through some double doors that had a staff only sign on there. Customers were staring as the security walked closely to us, ushering us to a room where they obviously take all the thieves. What the hell had I just done?

My heart was pounding, I had never been caught stealing anything before. I had no idea what the procedure was. Do I lie and say I'm someone else? Will they take me to the police station? I didn't know, I just knew that I was scared. Jade and I were told to sit down by the security man. "No" I said, continuing to pursue the 'bad gyal demeanour'. Jade looked up at me with evil eyes but still never spoke a word. She sat down, ready to do as the security man asked. "How old are you?" he asked. "14" I mumbled. "18" Jade replied after. Jade had to give her details because I was too young to be questioned and we both sat waiting for my dad to collect us from the store. Thank God, they never called the police.

Whilst waiting, I was role playing all the lies I could tell my mom and dad and it finally came to me, just like that.

"Jade put the tape in my pocket Dad." I told my dad after the silent journey dropping Jade back home. Well at least it seemed silent. I later came to realise my dad was cussing us out. Every swear word you can think of was used. Luckily for me, my dad never used to smack me when I was younger so I knew I was safe with him. "Seph, I'm going to stop taking you to your cousins, they're a bad influence on you." He snarled, with rage in his eyes. We were driving faster than usual so I knew that my dad was disappointed in me.

Not going back to my cousins? That's a bit far-fetched, I thought. That was the worst thing I could hear, tears started rolling down my face at that thought that I would never see my cousins again. My dad always seen the best in me and never believed I could do anything wrong, he never stopped blaming Jade for my theft, even up to this day.

"Tell the truth Seph, you can't let Jade take the blame," – there goes the voice in my head again. We pulled up to my house. Mom was waiting at the door, puffing on her cigarette looking vexed. I knew that she was far from happy but I had my story set, so in my head I wasn't to blame.

"Hello Mom." I tried breaking the ice. She was having none of it! My mom stood still and looked past me, she was humming a beat I had never heard her hum before. That was a sign of anger in my home. Anytime Mom was losing her patience, she would start to hum the beat to a song, after that song you would know that it was 'telling off' or 'beating' time. I walked past her, my dad following behind and on the stairs to my right was my uncle David sitting with a belt in his hands which was folded equally in two. He was making the two ends meet at a fast pace so I could hear the snap of the belt similar to a crocodile snapping. That indicated that I would be beaten with that belt as punishment. I was so scared, although it was common in my era to get beaten, by the time my mom and dad had me, their style of discipline changed which meant I escaped the beatings. On odd occasions, I would get a smack but nothing too heavy. I jumped to each snapping sound of the belt even though I knew exactly when the sound would occur. My uncle stared at me, grinning. "Do you know that what you just done was really bad?" He said. This was my chance to own up to my mistakes and just take the beating, after all, I deserved the punishment for stealing. Just before I could speak an image flashed in my head of me crying from the pain of the belt. I was not about to go down like that.

"I never do it, my cousin put it in my pocket." I vocalised. Shit! I failed again. What a b**ch! My poor cousin Jade, she done nothing but amazing things for me and treated me like her sister and I was making her out to be terrible. My dad stepped in with full protection mode and said "I've sorted it!"

"Sorted it? She done wrong, she needs to be punished." My uncle said angrily.

"It was not her, I have sorted it!" Dad shouted, the ego in him kicked in and he took full control of the situation. Yes! He saved me from a beating.

"I'm taking Seph back with me, I've just come to collect Grace." My dad made his way back to his car.

(Meet Grace: Grace is the closest one of my four sisters. We were only two years apart in age so we had our whole childhood together. She was my protector and role model. She had the perfect figure, a beautiful face, good skin, she was an amazing dancer and had everything going for her. She would always come to my dad's house with me, he treated her like a daughter).

I sat in the car bursting wanting to tell Grace the truth about the theft situation because I knew I could tell her anything. The journey back to my dad's house seemed longer than usual. We played our games in the car like eye-spy and we would hold our bellies going over the speed bumps as if we were on a rollercoaster. I could sense that Grace wanted to ask about the tape but she held it in and never mentioned anything.

When we arrived, we both ran to my room and sat on my bed. It was like an urge just waiting to come out, I told Grace everything. I knew that she would tell me exactly where I went wrong. She never judged me she just taught me things – my immediate teacher. I learnt so much from her; good and bad! Grace sat laughing in hysterics as I told her the whole truth and nothing but the truth. This made me feel a whole lot better for the fact that she could see the comedy in the situation. She was in tears from the amount of laughter when I told her what my uncle was doing with the belt. I felt so much better and suddenly what started out as a great day gone wrong was slowly going great again. It was still playing on my mind that I may not see my cousin Jade, and that she would be punished for my wrong doings. I needed to make it right. Grace suggested that we somehow get my dad's phone and pretend we were calling Mom but really, we would call Jade. That sounded great to me, so that is exactly what we done.

We called Jade's house in hope that one of the children would pick the phone up and not my aunty. Anxiously waiting after a few rings,

"Hello." Somebody picked up, I couldn't tell who it was I just knew it wasn't Aunty Carol, as she would always sound posh on the phone.

"Mya, is that you?" I aksed.

"Yes, it's me. How comes you said Jade stole the tape if it was you?" Mya shouted in anger. I couldn't blame her, she was just looking out for her little sister.

"Erm, I didn't know what to do, I was scared." I uttered. "My Uncle was going to beat me with the belt!"

I was feeling terrible at this point, I kept thinking about my cousins not liking me anymore because I had just got one of them into trouble by telling lies. I needed to actually speak with Jade.

"Well I will put Jade on the phone." Mya said. As she left, I could hear her in the background saying "Don't be soft with her Jade, she lied on you remember."

Jade came on the phone and never said anything at all, I could hear her breathing pattern, I assumed that she was very angry. It was silent for what seemed like forever.

"Hello Jade… I'm so sorry." I said in my most remorseful voice. Jade burst out laughing.

"Seph you are such a knob, you should have told me you were going to take a tape, a Damage one as well, I would have told you I got that album yesterday, look how you had me shouting at the security guard."

"I know, I should have said something to you, sorry for saying you took it though, I was going to get a beating. Did you get in trouble?" I asked, anxious to know how much of a mess I had caused.

"Oh no, don't worry about that, my mom never said anything because I told her the truth, she was cool. When are you coming back to mine?" Jade asked. This was great, Jade was not angry with me at all. In fact, she recited some of the security guard scene whilst laughing outrageously. We had a good laugh on the phone before I interrupted telling Jade, "My dad said I cannot come back to yours".

"That's just scare tactics, see you soon." Jade hung up the phone after a funny conversation and I was left with mixed emotions. I was just happy that she was ok with me and we were still best cousins. Grace told me that everything would be forgotten about and that I would be allowed back to my cousin's house very soon. After all, my dad and aunty were very close as brother and sister so they wouldn't have been able to keep away for too long.

She was right, I was back at Jades house which is where I started before I began telling you my theft memory.

My dad stayed strong for a few weekends and said that I could not go to my cousins but it was not long before I was back there doing what I loved to do on the block, hang out! That took a lot of begging, being sad and quiet visits to get me back there. But I made it! We spent the weekend jamming, eating good food and enjoying being kids. I was dreading going back home on Sunday, I had not sorted out my school uniform and I knew my mom was going to be upset again at the fact that I had left my uniform washing until Sunday evening. The fight for the washing machine in my house was absolutely crazy. With all those siblings and each of us washing our clothes separately due to the mix up of clothing garments, it wasn't easy. Mom always wanted our uniform washed on a Friday to save the hassle of rushing around on Monday morning but I was too lazy and too excited to get out the house that I made it my trend to do Sunday washing. I promised myself that I would become more organised one day- but I wasn't ready to take on that responsibility. Not just yet!

Lesson 1:

Patience- The present me!

By now you would have had a peek inside my life and a brief understanding of what family life was like for me growing up. In my earlier days, I always dreamed of writing a book as I found writing to be an expressive art in which I could step into my inner self and be free. At the age of 15 I wrote a beautiful poem for my mom and nan, it was written at a mother and daughters event which I was taken to by my youth workers. The poem was expressive of how I was feeling at the time and prior to that. In my teens, I went through mixed emotions about my mom, love, frustration, annoyance and anger. There would be times that I asked my mom to buy me things and the answer would be "No" with no explanation to follow and I would feel so hurt by that. I would ask if I could go places, stay over at my friends and all the other things that teenagers love to do but Mom would just say "No!" This wasn't all the time, but being a typical teenager, the times that my mom had told me no, I took it as a feeling of rejection and hate—she doesn't like me or else she would say yes—were the thoughts I used to have.

It was only when I became older and wiser that I realised that my mother was protecting me in the best way that she could. When she said no, it was because she could see some form of danger, wrong-doing or pain in the situation; or simply because she did not have it to give to me. If I understood that when I was younger I would have understood the importance of patience.

In life you will face temptations, things that appear to be easier and more comfortable to your life's routine at that precise moment.

But it is in the word 'No' that you can practice a form of patience. I used to find it hard to say 'No' to things that I didn't want to do or that I felt wouldn't benefit me in the long run. When I was asked to go places, or do something for a friend or family member, I would say "Yes!" Yes because it was easier to say, yes because it didn't come with any problems and yes because I was pleasing somebody.

But deep down inside, I knew that I wanted to say 'No' and I wanted to say 'No', without having to explain why, just as my mother used to do to me. This was really difficult but I learnt that, the people who love and care about you will honour you whether you say 'Yes' or 'No'. Learn to say 'No' as it will help you to become more patient and never feel like you have to explain why you are saying 'No'. When you say 'No' for the first couple of times it will feel very uncomfortable but that feeling dies down and saying 'No' will become as easy as saying 'Yes'.

At the end of each chapter in the book I will come back to the present me and inspire you by giving you tips, daily tools and lessons which will help you to feel roaring to go and start your new journey. I will tell you the exact methods I used to improve my mind in order to create the successes I have today. This I will assure you, can help towards finding or creating a better version of yourself, which only YOU CAN DO.

The first lesson that I want to touch on as you may have gathered, is **PATIENCE**.

Have you ever been in a situation where you really want something, I mean really want something, so badly that you have that exact thing that you want in your head. You envision it and correlate with it being yours but something else comes by quicker that is very similar and you get/take the thing that has come by quicker because you are done with waiting for that ultimate thing that you wanted to begin with? This can be with relationships, material things, a job opportunity or anything else that you can think of.

If you have answered yes, then you are suffering from NPS also known as the, 'no patience syndrome'. We have all done it in the past, where we have not been patient for something that would really benefit us, in exchange for something similar that comes along and fills the gap, the "make do" thing, many of us are guilty of it. And that's because we live in a fast, ever changing world and with social media being such a big influence on our world globally, it creates an urge for us where everything has to be had in an instant, right here, right now and makes it harder for us to be patient. Everywhere you look on social media there is something new, always a new challenge, new clothes, new ways to make money and new music. All of these things are just 'things' and these 'things' get replaced with new 'things' very quickly; but it creates a state of urgency. So, for the people who are trying to use a specific route to become successful but are side-tracked by the ever-changing media, they feel like they can never be successful because everything is always changing and everyone wants to be 'changing' in order to keep up. I call that 'The desire to be successful overnight.' This is impossible!

You cannot be successful overnight.

You can by chance win the lottery and become extremely rich, but being rich and being successful are two different things. Successful people make a difference in the world, they change people's lives, they create something for people to benefit from and they influence the masses. I don't need to go into what being rich is, as I'm guessing we all know that being rich is monetary gain only. Everyone wants to be successful overnight, they don't spend enough time practising what they are good at, they spend time changing themselves to fit into the trend within social media and get trapped in a cycle of doing what society wants them to do. Training yourself to be patient is very hard, especially if your someone who is very impatient and gets frustrated quickly, but it is possible.

Being patient, is accepting and tolerating the fact that there will be delays in your life which may sometimes occur in the most difficult times and circumstances. But you have to have the patience to deal with anything that life throws at you if you want to be successful, without getting angered, annoyed or even frustrated.

I'm guessing, if you're reading this book, you are seeking knowledge and motivation because you want better successes for yourself, and if you do, success requires you to be patient. It lives in the silent struggle that we have day in, day out of thinking that we are further away from our successes than we really are. If you want something really badly you have to be willing to push that extra mile to get it, even if it requires more time than what you planned. You have to be patient. Most of us, when we don't see that we have become successful overnight, we get distracted or we quit and the feeling of working so hard on something, putting your all into it and not seeing a single sign of success straight away, makes you want to give up.

We watch professional footballers, athletes, boxers, motivational speakers and other successful role models and see that they have huge followings, loads of money and an amazing lifestyle. We know that we would love the successes they have yet we don't take into consideration the work that needs to be put in prior to obtaining the results. We just see them at the top and think they got there in an instant, we ignore the time and years of practice that they have endured before getting there; which most successful people will have done.

Malcolm Gladwell, a speaker, author and journalist, spoke on a psychologist study in reference to patience which findings suggested that it takes 10,000 hours of practice at something in particular before you get good at it. Now, if that isn't some food for thought on how hard you have to work to make it to the top, then actually try doing the hours and noting them down. I can absolutely guarantee, that after 10,000 hours of doing what you love to do, you will be amazing at it.

A strong belief of mine is that; **ANYTHING THAT IS MEANT FOR YOU, WILL NOT PASS YOU.** Just have patience.

Now read that over and over again and digest it. You have to programme your mind to understand that, sometimes you have to wait a little longer to achieve something, wait a little longer to invest in property, wait a little longer to have children, wait a little longer to get married, wait a little longer to graduate and wait a little longer to find love. With that will come temptation, shorter routes to what you think can replace your initial desire and you will be tempted; tempted to run or to even fly down that road because you don't want to feel like you're being left behind. But you need to understand the power in patience and **stay in your own lane**. Do what you love and master it, forget about what everyone else is doing because they are not you. This will have you side-tracked and playing a game of catch up.

Slow and steady ALWAYS wins the race.

There is going to be time when you plan, and prepare yourself well, doing everything right but still fail to produce what you planned to do. You will encounter everything bad that you imagined could happen and you will feel like you have come to the end of the road! **DO NOT BE DISHEARTENED!** Keep on pushing until you have nothing left in you to give. It is sometimes at that exact point where you feel like it is all over, that with a bigger push, you were about to trigger something really big.

Maybe you set a goal for yourself that you did not achieve within the timescale, maybe all the friends you grew up with are professionals in the corporate world and you're sat at home with your children feeling under pressure that your life is not going anywhere because you are comparing it to what you can see others doing and thinking that you should be in the same position. Do not fail to take credit for the fact that you had to bear the child for nine months then deliver and be the child's teacher and nurturer. You may have missed the time to be a professional in the corporate world, but as long as you have breath, you have life. It is never too late to start something, you just have to be patient with yourself and know that whatever is meant for you will not pass you!

Life gets in the way of life and that is ok. If you research many of the successful figures in life, you will hear them talk about failing or being rejected at some point in their career. Sometimes things just don't go to plan but this isn't a warrant to quit what you're doing. It's a chance to start over and to keep on pushing through until the end. It's a way to learn from your mistakes and come back harder.

It's not about who starts the job. It's about who gets the job done!

In the chapter that you just read, I speak about stealing when I was younger. This was a common thing in my area and generally just a common thing for people that I associated with. Everyone was stealing from superstores because we didn't have the things that we wanted, or more so our parents couldn't afford to fund the daily things we portrayed as necessities. Instead of just waiting until I could afford the tape that I stole in the story above or just settling with the fact that I could not have it because it wasn't for me, I decided to rush the process and steal the tape only to realise that my cousin had it all along. Neediness and desperation got the better of me, so badly that it led me to commit a crime. Now, if I was older, I would have been prosecuted for theft and believe me there is nothing worse than losing TIME. As you get older you learn that the best things in life are worth waiting for.

In my neighbourhood, the motive was very simple – to work very hard for money! When I began educating myself financially I started to understand that the richest people in the world **make money <u>work</u> for them**. From a young age, I learnt about the hunger for success "the grind" we would call it, but it made me impatient and this continued into my adult life and had an effect on many things especially when I got into starting my own business. I just wanted everything NOW! I couldn't bear to wait for anything, not even a return from stock I had brought to sell, so I would let things and services go for less than the value of them, which worked at the time because I made a sale but in the long run failed me miserably because I wasn't making any money from the business. I was so impatient that I failed my business and you will read more about that in a later chapter. Luckily for me I had a bigger and greater belief in myself that I was not made to be poor and struggling and I wish for you all to have a greater belief in yourselves that will keep you going even when you encounter failures.

My belief kept me going, it took a lot of me practising things that would normally make me feel frustrated, and I kid you not, it was hard work but I found that, the more I practiced, the more comfortable I became. One day I came across a story that I heard Les Brown (A life coach and motivational speaker) talk about and it helped me practice patience so much that when I feel like I am becoming impatient (because you can always feel it, it's the feeling of being stuck and frustrated with life) I refer back to the story. I have decided to share it with you in hope that it will help you as it did me.

The story of the Chinese Bamboo Tree

You take a little seed, plant it, water it, and fertilize it for a whole year, and nothing happens.

The second year you water it and fertilize it, and nothing happens.

The third year you water it and fertilize it, and nothing happens. How discouraging this becomes!

The fourth year you continue to water and fertilize the seed and then---take note. Sometime during the fifth year, the Chinese bamboo tree sprouts and grows NINETY FEET IN SIX WEEKS!

Message: Allow yourself time to reach your mastery!

Chapter 2:

The Company You Keep

I was mid-sleep when I heard a constant ringing sound. I couldn't distinguish if it was a dream or reality, but I chose to go with dream as I was certain that I had just gone to sleep about half an hour ago. There was no possible way that this could have been the alarm on my phone – I thought as I lay there with the duvet covers over my head. I waited for it to stop but it didn't. I realised that my dream was now a reality; it was now time to get up. "Have I got to get up now?" I moaned to myself whilst making myself snugger in bed. I do this every time, the night before school I stay up chatting away on my Nokia to Tanya and then in the mornings I find it merely impossible to get up because I am so tired.

With the ringing continuing I reached for my phone from underneath my pillow and hit snooze with my eyes closed. I was so used to that button that I didn't need any vision to find it. But what time was it? Every night I would change my alarm time depending on the time I went to bed, I would sometimes give myself an extra 20 minutes. I slowly raised my left eyelid in hope to not take in too much light. But that was an epic fail. The big blue light on my phone had not gone off since I hit snooze and the time showing said 07: 36. "Argh!" I sighed with frustration before doing my full body stretch and whipping the crisp away from the corner of my eyes. I had to be out of the house by 08: 05 or else I would miss the 08: 10 bus. My school started at 08: 50 and was only a 10-minute bus journey away but the number 11 bus always took the piss especially when we had to let the George Dixon kids off. It would take 30 minutes to get to school on those days.

After taking my time to get ready and making sure that my hair was done it was time to leave, no breakfast, just out of the door. I had to prioritise out of the two, having breakfast or making sure that the hair gel was distributed correctly on my face in order to get little 'S' shaped squiggles at the front of my head. I always chose my hair, in fact I always chose anything besides breakfast. I was not a breakfast person. Which I later realised was a terrible thing for me. Mom was not home today when we were getting ready for school because she had a caring job which started around 6am in the morning, so two out of five mornings we had to be independent. Well, when I say independent I just mean we had no one shouting at us or directing us when to leave. I always got dressed quicker than Grace, she was a hygiene freak. I could never understand why she would take so long in the shower, I was fatter than Grace and even after washing every body part as slow as I could I was still always quicker than her and ready first. I left Grace in the house and made my way to Simone and Tanya's, who lived a 35 second walk away from me.

(Meet Tanya and Simone: Tanya and Simone were my closest childhood friends. We shared a connection from very young and became friends from around the age of 4. They knew everything about me and wouldn't judge me for anything that I had done; maybe because they were doing it also. It was rare that you seen one of them without me and me without them).

Simone and Tanya would take forever to get ready so I would always message them about 15 minutes before I left my house to say I'm outside in order for them to be outside when I got to them. They did not mind being late to places but I hated being late. The arrangement we had worked wonders and I left them to believe all those years that I was waiting outside for 15 minutes in the hope that they would feel guilty for their actions. They never did!

Each morning we would sing songs and speak about boys that we fancied on the way to school. Simone and Tanya went to a different school to me, but it was all on the same route so we would get the same bus. Tanya started her usual morning antics as we left to go to school and began singing away;

"I believe I can fly, got shot by the F.B.I..." She was remixing R-Kelly's hit single because she did not know the correct words.

"All I wanted was a chicken wing, from KFC or Burger King..." She would always sing that song in order to show off her vocal range, she believed that she could sing extremely well, as good as Beyoncé. Tanya's singing was terrible and although she knew we thought that, it never stopped her from expressing her voice day in day out. We used to get so much jokes just singing with one another, whether it was a sing off or just a casual song. To us, we sounded good and to Tanya, she sounded great.

I looked down the Aberdeen Street as far as I could see and seen the bus emerging, I shouted to Grace without even knowing if she had left the house or not "Grace run, the bus is coming!" Grace always made me late to school and I always had to wait for her because she was my older sister and my mom did not trust me going to school alone. If she was in the mood to be early then we would be but besides that we would just be late. Today was a good day as Grace came running up the street and all four of us ran for the bus.

The bus arrived at the stop before we did but had to let all the hospital workers off, so we were able to get on. There were no seats left for us to sit down on as the bus was still full. This was an everyday thing for the number 11 bus. It would arrive and would be jam packed, all seats occupied and people standing side by side, you can only imagine the stench in summer months. Yuk! We went upstairs to see if any seats were available and it was also full. "Forget it, we may as well just stand up here." I said to the girls. The girls agreed and we stood facing the direction the bus was travelling, holding on to one another in case the bus decided to jerk and throw us all face first on the bus aisle.

"Yo Seph." A deep voice shouted from the back of the bus. I tried peering past the two girls and guy that was stood in the way to see who was calling me,

"Seph it's me, Jay." He said.

"Oh hey." I replied, finally seeing him spread across the back seat.

"You lot come back here there's seats for you." Jay shouted. Trying to keep my balance, I tugged onto Tanya's jacket and told the girls that there were seats at the back. We started making our way to the back, walking past the envious faces that heard us get a seat offer. "Well there must not be seats available if they're standing." Said Simone. We took the risk anyway as we would have preferred to be sat down for the rest of the bumpy journey.

(Meet the clique: Skipper, Jay, Rico and Ryan. Four guys who I met in high school that became four brothers. We went to the same school and I learnt a lot from each of them individually growing up. I spent a big chunk of my life with them, in which we all still remain good friends).

Jay and Ryan were sat at the back of the bus on the long five-seater, taking up more seats with their school bags. That was perfect.

"Move over then." I said to Ryan as I shoved his leg out of the way so we could sit down.

"Where's Skipper and Rico?" Tanya asked.

"I spoke to Rico and he's with Skipper on Bearwood high street. They got on the earlier bus." Said Ryan. We all looked at each other surprised, as Skipper was never early for School.

I loved getting to school early because it meant that we could start our day with laughs which always made the day at school a lot better. On the bus, we were talking about what we would be doing this Friday after school and we decided that we would enter the haunted house that was located near to our school. Yes, you heard right, an actual haunted house. How deranged of us to even think about entering this property that said keep out. We all laughed speaking about the tactics we would use to get in there and all the crazy things we thought may be in the house. I had to somehow get out of going to my dad's house this weekend because I didn't want to miss out. Since going to secondary school, the weekend trips to dads turned into every two weeks and then even once a month. I had less time for my family; I just wanted to be on the streets playing out with my friends. Dad had a court order which I never understood as a kid, I just knew that I had to go to his house every weekend. But I wanted to hang out every weekend, especially when we were doing crazy stuff such as going to the haunted house! Dad never made me feel bad for not wanting to come to his house all the time, so the arrangement we had worked well.

The bus arrived near school and we all said our goodbyes to Simone and Tanya. We got off the bus to meet Rico and Skipper by the shops. Rico was eating a big bag of strawberry bonbons, he would put one in his mouth and throw another at one of us. Rico was a playful guy, he never took life too seriously and always found the humour in any situation – even if it was a serious one. I remember going to an after-school concert and I was acting the clown. A child was performing their piece on the stage and I was being very rude and talking loud when one of the parents of the children in the production turned around and told me to "Zip it!" I was going to get all street on him and give him a real piece of my mind but I had to humble myself because I knew I was in the wrong. Of course, my whole clique found that very amusing and laughed at me the whole day. Rico however, made fun of me every day for what felt like a month and made it difficult for me to speak. I would try and say a sentence and he would cut me off saying "zip it." He was such a punk at times but a punk that we all loved.

It was approaching 08.50 and we all had to go into school. This was the part I dreaded as I always loved being with my clique and I knew it was time to go and hang with people my own age and learn stupid shit about things that I was not interested in. I was seen as a smart kid in school, I was in all the top sets but I just found school lessons to be crap so I always started mischief in the lessons and had to let everyone know who was boss. I thought I was an actual gangster in school and so did my school friends, together we were unbeatable. The maddest, biggest and baddest girls and no one could mess with us.

(Meet TLC aka The Lordswood Crew: Paris, Hally, Charlene and Martina. I met these girls on day one of secondary school. All completely different characters that made up our crew, our motive was simple; give every teacher a hard time because they gave us a hard time).

I was friends with everyone in school as we were the popular group of girls but TLC were my girls that I was really close with. We rolled together every day at school and I still hang out with them up to this present day. They were just cool girls, from similar backgrounds to me and just understood me and I understood them. We were separated from each other in all classes except Spanish, because of the drama we used to cause in the lessons. The teachers would be left pulling their hair out when we were done with them.

Just this teachers luck!

Form was over and Spanish was on the agenda. Before going to class, we were messing about in the corridors, we were shouting, running and disturbing the other classes. We had to be in lesson but we were taking our time because we simply didn't care. Just as we got to the classroom door there was a slight anticipation as I felt that I could skip this lesson and stay in the toilets on my phone for the next 2 hours, that thought didn't last for long as Charlene pushed me into class and I fell onto the table.

Everyone in class was laughing including me. The supply teacher was astonished. Where was Miss Miller, our usual teacher? She must have been pulling a sicky because she knew that she had to teach us today. I was waiting for her to shout at us as she did every week when we entered the class in Seph and Charlene style. Miss Miller had tried for many weeks to get us separated but none of the other teachers would have us in the class. They had already moved us out of the top sets and we were now with the slow learners which made it even worse for the teacher because we had already learnt everything she was teaching us. Paris, Charlene, Hally, Martina and I pulled our chairs to sit down whilst laughing our heads off. The teacher looked pissed off already. She had no idea what was to come.

"Right girls you have missed the register so I will have to mark you down as late." Miss said with a very stern voice. To any average kid this would have been their queue to start behaving, however, we were not average so we did not care at all about what she was saying.

"Ha ha ha," Paris began laughing sarcastically which set the class off cracking up again.

"Is she for real?" Paris said as she took her time to take her stationery out of her bag.

No one was shocked by Paris' cheek towards the teacher as this was typical for Paris. She was known in school as the cheeky one. Very sharp with answers and had to be the last person to say something in an argument.

"Excuse me!" Miss said, looking extremely outraged by what she had just heard Paris say. I could not sit and let Paris have so much fun without me, it was funny to watch so I thought I'd better get involved before this teacher leaves. "Excuse me." I said in my most matching voice. You know when people say "If looks could kill?" Well this was one of those moments. I had determined in less than a minute that this teacher did not like me. Great, she will have to join the rest of them that felt the same way. I never understood why so many teachers did not like me, well that's what I believed for my whole journey through school. That made it ok for me to misbehave in the lessons because in the hood you were never nice to someone who doesn't even take the time to get to know you to determine if they like you or not.

I could see that Miss felt humiliated and for a slight second, I felt sorry for her. She began shouting at me and Paris and asked us to leave the class. She told us that we must report to the head teacher with a note she had written to explain why she was sending us out. Paris stood up in a flash, this day was getting better. We were not even 10 minutes in and already crappy Spanish was over. Hooray! I walked over to get the note out of the teacher's hand, when she slammed it down on the desk. "What a b**ch!" Muttered the little voice in my head.

"I hope that hurt." Came out loudly.

"Right, leave now!" Miss shouted. At this point I didn't think she could have been more angered until Paris replied saying "Ok ok, keep your hair on." The rest of the students became uncontrollable as some held their bellies in hysterics. I gave Paris a high five and we left the class like true tyrants. I knew that I was not going to give the note to the head teacher, how lovely of that new witch to trust me so much, clearly, she did not know me.

I went to my locker to get the sweets out that I had brought this morning. I knew that there may be some students passing in the corridor whether it was to go to the toilet or if they were just out of their lesson. I saw this as an opportunity to make money and could not pass up on it. Every morning that I was early to school I would stop off at the shop and buy sweets and drinks to sell to the other students in the playground. We were not allowed to sell things at school but I did anyway. I would buy a pack of sweets that had individual wrapped sweets in there for forty pence and then sell each sweet for like twenty pence. I would always treble my money at the very least, the entrepreneur in me had that all figured out.

I filled my pockets and pencil case with the sweets and went off to find my clients. After 20 minutes of hustling and making exactly £4.20, Paris shouted me to let me know that the teacher was coming. I tried stuffing the sweets that were left in my pocket into my pencil case and Paris began doing the same. We could hear Miss Ruby's heels clogging on the floor. Paris thought it would be funny to stick some up her jumper to make her boobs look pointed. Shit! We were definitely in trouble now. Not only were we sent out of class 22 minutes ago, we were also selling on school premises and Paris had now decided that it was a good time to take the mick.

Miss Ruby was now standing just a foot space away from us. "What are you ladies doing out of your class?" She asked us. I looked over at Paris to see the sweets poking out of her jumper creating a triangular boob. I sniggered as I could not hold back the laugh. "Erm! Miss just sent us out for no reason." I said, knowing that there was no possible way she would believe that. I heard something hit the ground. Paris had let go of holding her jumper and all the sweets had fell out on the floor. Miss Ruby only had to look at us and we knew exactly what the outcome would be. Isolation!

She sent us both to isolation whilst banging on about how disappointed she was in us. She told us that we would never amount to anything and that the teachers are wasting their time with us. This was common language from most the teachers in the school. I remember when it was telling Seph "She will not become anything," week. I had heard it so much in one week that I told my friends that the teachers were plotting against me and that they had all planned to say it as part of a prank. The prank was never revealed that was just something that the teachers done. I started to believe that school was just a coping mechanism, I came to school for my friends and not for education.

Isolation was empty as it was still very early in the morning. Miss Ruby had to find a teacher to look after us whilst we were in there. We were given a single line to write as many times as we could in one hour. 'I will not misbehave in class and I will try my best at all times'. What were these teachers getting out of us writing the same line over and over again? Was it to improve our handwriting? That's all it seemed to do. That was a ridiculous method of punishment but I knew that I would try beating my last week's personal best of 5 lines in one hour. I'd ought to go for six or seven today as I was feeling generous.

As soon as Miss Ruby left, me and Paris began laughing and relaying the events that had just happened. We spoke about all the possible outcomes with the worst being the teachers telling our mothers about our behaviour. Paris' mom was very similar to mine and as much as we misbehaved in school we did not want our parents to find out how we were behaving at school or else we would have been in trouble. The respect we had for our parents growing up was too large for a teacher to destroy what we had worked all our 14 years to build.

Twenty minutes into isolation and no teacher had arrived, another one of my friends came strolling into isolation, she was the year above us her name was Camille. Camille was the nicest of her year group and always showed us love when we were at school. She would be in the playground teaching us things that we needed to know about the teachers and how to do things and get away with it at school.

"What are you in for?" I asked her as if we were completing a ten-year prison sentence.

"Oh, just for being a bit chatty in the class." She replied.

"That cannot be it, you wouldn't be sent to isolation for being chatty in the class." Paris said.

"It's the things I was talking about babe." Camille smirked as she said that. I knew what was coming next after she said that.

"Was you talking about sex?" I asked her. She laughed and replied;

"Well you know me Seph, I was just educating some classmates as the teachers did not want to do it for us." We all giggled and began chatting away. The cover teacher arrived and looked horrified when she saw me in there. Out of all the teachers they could have got to cover the class they got Miss Moore.

(Meet Miss Moore: Out of the twenty plus teachers I had, Miss Moore was the only teacher that expressed that I could become something in life. She saw past what it said about me on paper and was interested in what my life purpose was and how she could help me along my journey. She pushed me to succeed throughout school and always made me work extra hard even in lessons that she was not teaching. Miss Moore was the reason to why I made it out of school with 14 GCSE's A*-C grade).

"Morning Miss Moore." I said. Miss Moore did not look happy. Paris and Camille sat up straight in their chairs, greeted Miss and began writing their lines.

"Put them pens down." Miss sounded disappointed in us. "Why are you girls back in here, am I wasting my time talking to you about why school is so important?" None of us answered, assuming it was a rhetorical question. "Well, am I?" she shouted.

"No Miss Moore!" We all said in unison.

"Listen to me and listen good as I will not be repeating myself again!" Miss Moore was upset.

She went on to lecture us on the importance of getting an education in order to become successful and have a good job when we were older. She told us that we could be anything that we put our minds to and that we just had to work slightly harder coming from the neighbourhoods that we were raised in. She also said that we had to stay out of trouble's way until we created a platform where trouble would not find us. Miss Moore had a theory that if you made yourself accessible to trouble and behaved how the other teachers expected you to behave, then you would somehow become what the teachers were saying you were. She called it self-fulfilling prophecy. We sat listening to her until our hour was over and left the class.

Just as we were leaving isolation Charlene was on her way to isolation. She too, had be sent out of Spanish for misbehaving. Charlene was swinging her bag around by the strings and had no care in the world and always enjoyed isolation better than her classes. I pushed into her to get her back for my terrible fall this morning but she managed to escape falling over. "See you later kiddo, enjoy isolation." I said to Charlene using a sarcastic tone.

After spending the day reflecting on what Miss Moore had to say, the school day was finally over. Yay! I met Charlene in the corridor at 3: 30pm and we waited for my sister Grace to walk out of school. I took my Nokia phone out to turn it off silent. As I looked at my phone I saw five missed calls and seven messages. The calls and texts came from Simone and Tanya. At this point I thought that it must have been an emergency to why they were ringing me during school hours. I didn't have any calling credits so I could only message them to tell them to call me. Before they called me, I opened the message off Tanya that read "Come to my school, drama". Suddenly my phone began to ring and it was Simone. She was yelling about some girls at her school that had been talking some shit about her.

Simone sounded angry and said that she was going to fight one of the girls. Now I knew immediately that if a group of girls were there in person, there was no way that they would have let them fight one-on-one. I told Simone that I was on my way and told the girls about the drama. As I was telling my sister and Charlene what had happened, Paris and Martina were approaching the bus stop. They could see that I was angered from the shouting and hand gestures I was using to simply explain the texts. They said that they were coming along in hope that we would out-number the girls at the other school. We all left to go to Simone's school.

When we got half way through the journey we saw the bus that Simone and Tanya were on and could see a lot of confrontation going on. The upstairs of the double decker bus was filled with girls in Green uniforms. I noticed Simone because she had bright pink braids in her hair. We all began chasing the bus, the driver obviously thought that we were innocent girls trying to get home, so he pulled over at the bus stop and waited for us to get on. Shit was about to go down!

I was actually excited to be fighting again so near to my last fight which was just last week when I proved to myself that I was somewhat of a hard knock. I walked up the stairs with the adrenaline pumping through my body. I had no idea about what had been spoke about previous to us arriving I just knew the face of the girl who was talking crap about Simone. I made my fists into a ball and began to fight. All of the girls began fighting and what started off as a pleasant journey for some passengers, ended as one big brawl of a nightmare. It was over so quick, I heard the driver on the phone to the police telling them to come and arrest us all. I started to feel the same emotions as I did when I stole the tape. If I got arrested I would be punished! Punished more than the beating that I had escaped from uncle David for stealing. I had to disappear fast! One of the girls pressed the emergency exit open on the bus as the driver tried to keep us there until the police came. We all ran out of the exit, even the girls that we were just fighting. It was so strange because there was no real issue between us and the other girls, so once the fight stopped we all made our way home.

It was 5: 15pm when I arrived home and mom had asked us why we had taken so long to get back. I told her about the fight in major detail but failed to tell her that I was involved. She began yelling saying that I needed to stay away from trouble and that I could have been dragged into the incident and maybe got hurt. As she was rambling on my inner gangster ego kicked in;

"Mom – me, get hurt?" I laughed as I said it as if I was untouchable. I was brought back to reality with a clip around the ear.

"Ouch, that hurt Mom." I said. The joke turned on me and now my older sister Fiona was laughing too. Fiona was helping my mom to share out the food and whatever was cooking smelt absolutely delicious. My mom was an amazing cook and always enjoyed making delicious home cooked meals, it was not evident at dinner time that we were a poor family because a little always went a long way. I went upstairs to change my school uniform in a hurry and came back downstairs to see that my mom had made roasted barbeque Chicken with my favourite rice and all the trimmings. Fiona had laid each plate out on the kitchen surface and began to fill them. I already knew in my head which one was mine, the one that was filled the most, I looked at my plate and knew that the food did not have much time left on there, I danced around the kitchen excited to eat whilst getting the sauce and my fork. When I turned around, the plate I assumed was mine was no longer there. In fact, no other plates were there. Why was Fiona trying to wind me up? Surely this must have been a joke.

"Who has taken my food?" I shouted. No-one replied so I decided to turn the volume up a notch and ask again to ensure that all my siblings heard. I had a feeling that it was Fiona as she made a habit of sharing out the food plates incorrect, there was always one less or one more, hardly ever the correct amount. This was a common problem in our house and I usually fell victim to having less food. My family sat in the living room eating their food, some on the sofas some on the floor and still no-one answered me. I was not about to serve my own food as I found this unfair, nor did I want the remains of the dinner that was left at the bottom of the pot. I went into 'immediate strop zone' and got my shoes on and left the house slamming the door. I was at Tanya's gate when I realised I had left my money and I was not going back, not after the tantrum I just threw. How would I even buy food from the chip shop with no money?

I knocked Tanya's door and asked if she was coming out. Me and Tanya hung out every day after school. Our playing out days were not weather permitted, we went outside come rain, sun, snow, hail and wind. We just wanted to be outside. Tanya's mom Sharon opened the door and greeted me with a smile.

(Meet Sharon: Mom no.2. She was not my biological mother but an educational mother that I learnt some life lessons from. She was a teacher in the corporate world and had been to university so I saw her as a positive role model).

"Hi Sharon"

"Hello Seph how are you?" she said as she walked back inside the house. I followed behind as that gesture usually indicated that I should come in and replied saying; "I am good thank you". Sharon was always very welcoming, she always had a smile on her face and spoke with a gentle tone. Most Christmas' she would count me in as one of her children on the table, I would have my own seat and be treated as Tanya and her siblings were. Sharon was a teacher with six children. She always spoke about life in a different way to what my mom did. I used to enjoy listening to all her stories and tried remembering the little details so that I could learn from her. Just like my dad, she owned a house so I knew that by listening to her stories I could learn a few things and maybe even apply them to the social work system. She would ask me what I wanted to become in life every time I saw her which put pressure on me to always have an answer that I thought she would be proud to hear. I adopted Sharon as my second mother, not by law but in my head, I had two mothers.

I went upstairs to see what Tanya was doing, as I opened her door she was practising the dance routine that we had just learned last Thursday at dance class. She was dancing to the sound of her own voice and was singing a B2K song. I laughed and suggested that she played the actual CD in order to get each move right to the correct beat. I asked Tanya to come to the chip shop with me and told her what had happened with the food situation, she agreed to lend me some money and we made our way to the shops.

"Chilli and Mayonnaise please" I said to the lady that had just served my large kebab meat and chips. I could smell the vinegar in the air and became excited to finally eat some food. For a minute, I was upset that I had missed out on my favourite rice, but chips were my favourite thing to eat so I was content. As soon as we left the shop I ripped open the paper and began walking in the direction of my home scoffing my face. I had no fork and my hands were filthy but I had a much better way of cleaning them; I sucked my fingers off to make sure I had all my £3.00 worth of the meal. Tanya ordered a scallop as she only had 20p in change, this was a large chip in a circular shape with extra batter.

We saw Skipper on his bike riding to the chip shop, he asked us to wait for him whilst he ordered his usual chicken breast and chips. We took what was left of our food and went to Summerfield park to hang out. After about 8 minutes of sitting on the top of the slide graffitiing the house-like apparatus with "Seph was here" we decided that we were bored and that we wanted to do something more fun. We all walked back to Skipper's house so that he could put his bike away as Tanya suggested that we go on a bus ride to get lost. Skipper lived close to my house and hung out with me and Tanya most days. He put his bike away and we were off wherever the wind would have taken us. It was 6: 30pm, I was not confident that we could get lost and find our way back home before school tomorrow morning. Our mothers would not accept that at all. I know that my mom would kill me if I stayed out without asking, especially after leaving the house in such a strop.

The bus arrived and we got on and waited until it took us into an area that we didn't visit much. We then started hopping on and off random busses until the journey home was untraceable. The situation was out of my hands now, I was terrible with directions so I literally had no idea of how we would get back. I had to trust that Tanya and Skipper would get me home safe. I wasn't anxious, in fact at that precise moment I was hoping that we couldn't find our way home until the next morning because then I would miss school. The bus pulled up at a bus stop in an area that looked strange, there were two pubs located very near to one another and both had England flags hanging out of the window. Skipper asked me and Tanya if we knew where we were, we said no. I assumed that Skipper had secretly known as he asked us in a tone that suggested that he knew. We got off the bus and decided to stroll the streets in this random area. Across the street was a guy with ripped blue jeans, white trainers and a red England top. He was holding a pint of beer and would not take his eyes off us.

"What the hell is he staring at? Weirdo." Tanya and Skipper laughed as my inner gangster kicked in. "Can we help you sir?" I shouted to sustain the amusement of them both. The man could see from my facial expressions that I meant business. All we did was show up and he was giving us the evils. What was this guy's problem?

"What did you say?" He shouted back."

"Why are you looking at us, do we have something for you?" I muttered. I never thought to analyse the situation at hand, we were in an area that we were unfamiliar with, there was a strange man drinking a beer and two pubs potentially filled with strange men.

"Come over here and say that you little nuisance." The man put his beer on the floor as if he were about to do something crazy. At this point Tanya was laughing hysterically. Skipper told us not to worry and said that we would all be ok. That was my queue to stop but the little voice in my head felt that it was the perfect time to keep me going in gangster mode.

"You're the nuisance, you flipping weirdo." I shouted as I raised my arms, to show that I wasn't scared. The man left his drink on the floor and went back into the pub. I started to flaunt to Tanya and Skipper as if I had just conquered the war and we carried on with the journey.

"Oi!" We heard someone shouting, less than one-minute later. This area started to seem stranger than the man we had just saw.

"Skipper, do you know where we are?" Tanya asked. It seemed as though she had similar feelings to me about the area. Skipper replied with a smirk on his face, "No, you lot said you wanted to get lost so that's what we are doing."

"Oi you!" The voice emerged again. Tanya looked behind and said it was the man that I had believed I conquered just minutes before. I never for a second believed her as I thought that I had scared that weirdo off, I did not even look back to check. Skipper looked behind and shouted "RUN!" Skipper always ensured that we were safe as he was the only guy with us on most days, so I knew that we had to run. I looked behind to see about 7 men of different sizes, all weird looking running towards us. My heart started pounding, the gangster in me was not being as present as I needed it to be. I had no time to think about what was going to happen, I just knew that I had to get away from these weird people. My belly was turning and the kebab meat and chips that had not digested properly felt like it was about to surface. The guys continued to chase us for what seemed like a lifetime. We managed to run onto a bus that was approaching, panting and out of breath. When we got to the back of the bus and sat down, it was seconds before any of us could speak, we seen the men running as fast as they could but Tanya had already told the bus driver that we were in danger. I had not laughed so much in my entire life. Skipper and Tanya were laughing and trying to piece together sections of what had just happened, I couldn't understand anything they were saying. We had to change buses a few times before getting back to our area but we did manage to get a bus that brought us directly back home in the end. This was a sign from the heavens; it was time for me to go home before I got into any more trouble that day. Our little lost adventure was so dangerous but we had so much fun. I knew that I couldn't tell my mom what had happened.

I pushed the key in my front door and went straight up to Grace's room. I had decided that I wasn't going to speak with Fiona nor my mom because they had not checked on me with a single phone call to see if I had eaten. I lay on the floor in Grace's room because she wouldn't let me sit on the bed without having a shower.

"Get off my floor" she said.

"Why?" I asked, confused to why she was shooing me out of her room.

"You smell like outside, go and have a shower". Grace had decided that I now needed to be clean to even lay on her floor.

"Whatever." I muttered. I left Grace's room as I was too exhausted to shower and went in my room to lay on my bed. All I could think about was the array of crazy ass events and dangers that had happened that day. Thank God, I had made it home safe, I had put myself in two high risk situations where I could have been locked up or killed but I wasn't bothered about any of it. This was just like any other day in the hood, I had to be entertained in some way, right?

Lesson 2:

Nurture good relationships and
let go of bad ones!

The people that you surround yourself with everyday have to be an **addition** to your life in a positive way. It is so important to identify the people that are there for you only through your successes and people that are there for you when you encounter failures and hard times. Learn to separate people that add light to your life from the people that take light away from your life.

When writing this book, I hand-picked the individuals in my life that were very influential to me and that impacted my journey to becoming the woman I am today. I don't go in depth about them all but I give you an insight to how they impacted me.

My mother, Valerie Martin, since I can remember has supported me with every decision that I have made since being an adult. She allowed me to make my own mistakes and learn from life without protecting me in a way that she did when I was a baby. This helped me to mature and grow. If you are lucky enough to have a great connection with somebody with more wisdom than you, that can teach you about life and be related to you, then you need to cherish that person. It is in those relationships that you learn to become strong. It's not having someone there to say yes to everything you ask, or to not say things in case it hurts your feelings. It's finding joy, in the realism of that person. They tell you exactly how it is, even if you do not want to hear it. That for me, is one form of a good relationship.

A good relationship will mean different things to different people and will usually consist of; teamwork, loyalty, balance, compromise, care and financial gain (business). In most cases each individual person in your life will have a different relationship with you. You just have to make sure that the people that you choose to invest your time and energy in, are GOOD PEOPLE WITH GOOD INTENTIONS AND GOOD ENERGY.

The hood has the most haters!

A hater is defined as: a critical or negative person who greatly dislikes life and does not want the best for you. They are sad and in a dark place and they try very hard to get everyone in the same space that they are in. BADMIND PEOPLE!

Now, the definition above is my personal definition of a hater, written in a way in which I hope you all understand. The hood is full of haters, people that do not want you to succeed and people that want you trapped in the hood with them. They will come in the form of family, friends and loved ones. Of course, there may be a few people who don't like you for no reason, who are just straight up haters, but the ones harder to identify are the ones closest to you. It can sometimes take a long time to distinguish these haters as the love you feel from them is very real, so you won't necessarily know that they are haters, until you encounter a situation that is new to you both and that person doesn't want you to elevate for all the wrong reasons. Most people will have haters around them that they have not yet identified, this is where I come in to help.

If any of the statements below sound familiar enough to be able to put a name to the statement, then that person you named is a HATER! Dispose of them fast!

- Every time you tell this person that you have a new idea or that you want to make a change in your life, they tell you that you are crazy and try to persuade you to follow the "normal" life and do what society wants you to do. **HATER!**

- This person listens to your ideas but only gives you negative feedback and then compares your idea to another that they tell you is better. **HATER!**
- This person smiles to your face about your idea and then negatively criticises it behind your back. **HATER!**
- This person tells you that you are not good enough to make it work because of the person you are. **HATER!**
- When you tell this person your idea, they start to talk about themselves and ask why you are not thinking about helping them into doing what you are doing. **HATER!**
- This person encourages you to go in the wrong direction because it's with them. **HATER!**
- This person really does genuinely want the best for you, BUT, does not want you doing better than them. **HATER!**
- This person is never happy for you when you tell them something you expect them to be happy about. **HATER!**

"Show me your friends and I'll tell you who you are"

This statement is very true and means exactly what it says. The people that you choose to spend your time with, the people that you hang around with will show the exact person that you are. If you are hanging around with people that don't want anything from life, or people that have a negative mindset... Then guess what? You become the person they are. The beauty in this statement is; that it works for the good. If you want to be successful, you have to find people, seek the good people out, be around people that know more about what you want to do, than you do. Be around people that have done well in something similar and can relate to your purpose. Find these people, they are out there. Even if it takes going to meet-ups and just speaking with someone new that can relate to you. It's all about adding new WINNING people to your team and cutting off those bring no value to your life.

I know this can be hard in the hood because you start to form friendships that turn into family, "he's my boy, she's my girl". But reality is, sometimes these people are no good for you and need to be set free in order for you to progress further in life. Spend time with loved ones, people that really want the best for you no matter if you're doing better than them. Choose your circle of friends wisely because **you are who you hang around with**.

When I was younger, I ended up in particular situations because of the people that I was around and the perception of what I thought 'being cool' was. Sometimes it would be peer pressure. I would do things that I knew was wrong just to fit in. And I knew it was wrong because I always had the gut feeling which I chose on most occasions not to follow. But I am urging you to follow your gut instinct and do what is right as it's usually a guide to keep you out of harm's way.

They say the five people that you spend the most time with will not only become your future but become your wage, your success and your mindset. The friends I mention in the story are still my best friends to this very day and it's not because of the amount of time I have known them for, it's the type of people they are. We all move together as a unit and support one another to become better people. I have had many friends, associates and acquaintances that have come into my life, we have made good memories, but they have not stayed in my life. That's not because they are all bad people but it's more because they do not add anything to my life and maybe I didn't add anything to theirs. Some people will come into your life for shorter periods than others, some will come into your life to teach you something you need to learn for the person you are going to become, but don't get hung up on holding on to "bad friends" and people that serve you no purpose just to say "oh I have many friends". You need to value your life more than that. If your friends are not doing any good for you, then you surely need a new set of friends. It's destructive to spend your time with people that sit and gossip, or always moan about life, or do not have any dreams, or any ambition, because in hindsight, you will become that same person I just described.

So, if I were you, I would firstly go through your phonebook, WhatsApp and messages. Who are the people that you are speaking to on a daily basis? Write them all down on paper. Next to their name, write down what they add to your life (POSITIVE AND NEGATIVE). Then start to filter through the good people and bad people. To do this task properly, you have to be 100% honest with yourself. And by the end of the task you will have a clearer insight into who is good for you and who is not. It may be that your whole phonebook is full of people that add nothing to your life, in that case you need to create a new phonebook.

Task 2: THE FILTERING PROCESS

I want you to spend the next 10- 15 minutes going through your call log and messages in your phone. On a blank piece of paper, I want you to write down the names of all the people that you have had contact with this week—there may be people you want to list that you don't speak to on the phone but you have a great relationship with—note them down also. All the people's names that have appeared more than twice, put a star by their name on the paper.

Next, only thinking about the names of the people with stars by them, I want you to think about how they make you feel. On a scale of 1-7 (1 being not so good and 7 being great) I want you to give each person a score. You have to be totally honest with yourself, even with family members. Go ahead and do that task now.

Now that you have scored each person, I have created 5 lines for the **best people.** Anyone that scored above a 6, put their names down in the space provided below and write one thing next to their name, that makes them a good person, to you. What is it that you like about them?

1)

2)

3)

4)

5)

These are your 'good people'. Always remember that when you are feeling down, when you need help, when you become successful and when you need direction. Show gratitude to those five and if you do not have any on the list or maybe as little as 1, then do not worry. You can meet new people and form new relationships that will benefit you and your growth. There are sites such as *LinkedIn* that enable you to meet the people that you require meeting.

It doesn't matter if you have not made it yet, you can still surround yourself with people that add value and positivity to your life. As long as you are all striving together to become better, then, you are around the right people. Everyone in your circle has to be winning, if you are the smartest person in your group, or the one that makes the most money, you need a new set of friends. You cannot strive for more when you know or earn the most, this is simply because your vision will not get you there without seeing the signs of possibility.

Millionaires hang out with millionaires. Hundred-aires also hang with hundred-aires and that's one of the most crowded, cluttered spaces. You wouldn't see a millionaire hanging with a hundred-aire unless that hundred-aire has levelled up and has the vision to become the millionaire. I hope I am making sense to you.

CHOOSE YOUR CIRCLE OF FRIENDS WISELY!

You need to have people around you that love you unconditionally, no matter if you are having the best day of your life, or the worst day. People that are so into you that when they see you fall, they jump to catch you, they rescue you in your time of need and they celebrate with you in your time of success. People that you can place your trust in, your trust to tell you when you are wrong as well as right. Everyone needs at least one of these people in their life. If you feel you have found a person like this, hold on to them and never let them go.

Message: "You cannot surround yourself with blindness and expect to see" T.D Jakes

Chapter 3:

Enjoy Your Childhood Whilst It Lasts!

Last night was a flipping tragedy. That's all I could think about whilst I slowly got out of bed to get ready for the day. Some of the girls went out, and what started off as an excited bunch of girls, turned into a screaming set of girls, running terrified for their lives. "Was this really going to be my life?" I questioned as I sat looking in the mirror at myself. Not if it had anything to do with me.

We met up around 6: 30pm yesterday and started getting ready at my house for the under 18's rave. I didn't have to lie to mom anymore when I went to the raves, like I first used to at the age of 11. I guess she let me go because she knew that I would have found a way to go anyway. All the girls were looking forward to it, as the superstar Monster Boy was in town performing his hit single – Sorry. We sat at the cassette player and memorised the words, using the rewind and pause buttons making sure that we never missed anything out and when we finally got it, we started to get ready for the rave.

I still couldn't believe what had happened. I grabbed my phone to call Tanya to talk about it, she wasn't answering so I kept calling until she answered. Grace was in the bathroom having a shower and I knew that I would have had to wait about 30 minutes just to discuss yesterday's events. After the fourth ring, Tanya finally picked up;

"Tanya, what the hell happened last night, we could have died" I said with a slight sense of laughter. I was laughing, still in shock.

"Seph, one minute we were dancing, having fun and the next

minute we were running out of the exit trying to survive, why were people letting off shots in the rave?" Tanya said.

If I knew the answer I would have told her. We sat discussing the events with gratitude that we were still alive and talking to each other. For the very first time I experienced a "that could have been me" moment. We were literally all having fun partying, when we heard gunshots fired inside the venue. Everyone was screaming, dropping to the floor for safety and running in a crazy state of panic. My initial reaction was to run in any direction. Grace grabbed my arm and we headed the way that the other girls were heading. As everyone was huddled together all trying to get out, I could see that the exit we were heading towards had become very smoky. I thought there must have been a small fire, but realised as I started coughing that it was a different type of smoke, I was finding it hard to breathe when someone shouted; "it's CS gas!". I used the bandana I had on my head to cover my mouth and had to go through the exit anyway to get outside.

When we got outside and thought that we were clear of everything we heard more gunshots fired. I could have sworn we were safe, obviously not. The running began again, this time a girl running beside us was hit in the leg and fell to the floor. We kept on running, something inside of me felt bad for being so helpless but it could have been me and I wasn't ready to be gunned down. I was so scared. Eventually we had run so far that we were about a mile away from the event, no taxis would pick us up because they must have heard the news about the gunshots, we were close to being stranded but managed to get a lift in the end. I was just happy when I was home and in my bed. I put my music on to aid me with getting ready for the day ahead.

It was a typical Sunday afternoon and mom was cooking up a storm. She had the barbeque out and had invited all the family around to come and eat. All my cousins, aunts and uncles came to fill their bellies and drink alcohol. We were out in the back garden with the music blasting, some of the family were conversating with each other whilst me and Grace were doing a dance routine. Grace and I loved to dance but she was always the choreographer, she was teaching me the classic routine to BellBivDevoe – Poison. I was so slick with my moves, I really got into character and put my all in when it was time to show the family what we had been practising. They all grabbed their food and gathered around like they were watching a movie at the cinemas. Skipper was controlling the music and I had signalled to him to start the track from the beginning as we were ready to show everyone what we were made of. The track started, it was a showdown, after striking a few poses, the vocal came in and we were off, hands in the air, knees up, I knew that we looked amazing doing the routine, I could tell by my family's reaction. Mom had got off her chair midway through our routine as the door bell was constantly ringing. When we finished, the family clapped and some of them started to join in, dancing to the music that was on, we all laughed and had so much fun. Sunday barbeques were a reminder of how amazing I thought my family were. I always invited the clique around on Sunday's as they were just part of the family. They had all come over today for their usual round of Sunday dinner and games of black jack, normally it would just be Skipper and Tanya but today it was a full house. It was a feel-good feeling and the day was going perfect until mom called me.

"Seph, what have you done?" she said, I could tell from the tone of her voice that she required an answer from me. Did I leave the stove on? I questioned myself, but being typical Seph, I shouted that I had robbed that bank I always spoke about, set it off style. The family began laughing at my carefully thought out joke. I always had everyone cracking up with my humour. However, I noticed that Mom was not smiling, she silenced me when she shouted;

"Come inside, the police are here for you".

A part of me thought that she was role playing with me but her face told me otherwise. What the heck was she talking about? This must have been a joke. My whole family sat in awe. I thought my mom was messing around even though she did not look as if she was. The little voice in my head appeared again letting me know that I had messed up big time, but it still was not piecing together the situation I had been in as to why the coppers were here for me. I ran through the list of "bad girl behaviour scenarios" that I had been involved in and they all appeared clean. I had professionalised my stealing skills and wouldn't steal anything serious anymore, just sweets and food, so I knew that there was no way theft had come back to haunt me – it wouldn't have been worth it. The corner shop that we had terrorised a few weeks back by locking the owner of the shop inside at open times using his shutters; seemed ok after we left so it couldn't have been him snitching on us. I continued to try and suss it, with nothing being clear.

But before I could get into my house the officer had come outside to arrest me, my family and friends were in shock and after a slight moment of silence they all jumped up to find out what was going on. Uncle Jelphy was under the influence of alcohol and had been on the wrong side of the law in the past. He jumped up in defence mode and stepped in front of me telling the officers they had to get through him first to get me.

Not again!

The scenario where my cousin Jade had protected me, instantly came back to mind. I was not about to let someone else get in trouble because of me, it was time to own my wrong-doings. "It's ok uncle Jelphy, I'll be fine." I said, as I stepped in front of him to make it easier for the officer to arrest me.

I looked at my friends puzzled to why I was the only one being arrested, after all, this was the clique, we had done everything together. They should have been handcuffed too. The officer started reading my rights to me. I wasn't talking much as my mind was doing overtime thinking of all the ways that I could get out of this scenario. My mom looked filled with emotions, I didn't know if she was angry or scared, I just knew that she required some answers from me. How dare I embarrass her in front of the family?

"Why am I being handcuffed?" I asked the police woman calmly. This was the first time that I had been in trouble with the police, their exaggerated arrest putting me in handcuffs looked really bad in the eyes of my family and made me look like a naughty child.

The officer told me that they had reason and evidence to believe that I was involved in a serious bus brawl. "Are you kidding me?" I shouted. The bus fight, that happened a couple of months ago was back to haunt me and I did not even hit that chatty mouth girl more than 4 or 5 times. I was fuming, all of this humiliation in front of my family for a little stupid fight. I asked my mom to come to the station with me after apologising to the family. Uncle Jelphy was still flaring up as he believed that all his nieces were angels.

"Don't worry uncle, I have to go with them." I told him. My uncle seemed to have sobered up really quick because the questions that he was firing at the police made me feel like he was the world's best lawyer or maybe he had memorised what questions to ask from his previous arrests. He followed me until I got into the car, I said goodbye to my family, most of them looking so scared for me like I was on my way to do a ten-year prison sentence.

"I'll be fine."– The bad girl in me kicked in. I reassured them that things were going to be ok. I was ready to do this sentence just so that I could come out of prison and earn more respect. Mom was sat in the car with me shaking her head and said that she will have to call my dad to let him know what had happened. "No, not my dad!" I pleaded. How would I explain to my dad that his princess had been fighting? I couldn't think of any excuse this time as my nerves were getting the better of me and I decided that I would tell my dad the truth.

"She hit me first Dad, it was self-defence." I said, when my mom past me the phone. There I go again, lying, just like I did with my cousin and the Damage tape. "Don't worry princess, everything is going to be ok." My dad said, he sounded like he was trying to prevent me from being scared to go to the police station. Dad didn't know that I was a street kid, the police didn't scare me. I knew that he had believed my story so I had to work on getting rid of all the anxiety that I had built up based around telling him the truth. Dad couldn't come to the station as he was working away, which was a blessing for me as I didn't have to lie to his face.

When I arrived at the station I saw Charlene's mom, she hadn't noticed me yet and was fiddling with the tv guide left on the tables, maybe she had a new job working in the police force, then I saw Charlene, it was a sense of relief that I was no longer in this alone.

The police made sure that me and Charlene had no contact by sitting us at separate sides of the station but I somehow managed to make eye contact with her and have a big mind conversation. I knew that Charlene and I had a similar thought process and we had previously had so many conversations about what to say if we were ever to get arrested.

After hours of being in the cold and smelly cell, it was time to go home. The police should have known that they wouldn't get any answers from me. I was a trained professional, similar to the Russian Spy you see in the movies and to top it off I was from Winson Green. I learnt from the hood that the best and quickest way to get out of the cell is to say "No comment!" To every question asked! And that's exactly what I did. I heard my solicitor telling my mom when I had to come back to court. It was only a week away! I couldn't wait to get home so that I could call Charlene to speak about it all. I had done much worse things than fight and now I had to go through all of this for what I seen as a minor hiccup. This was too time consuming and the only thing on my mind was, we never gave the girls from Tanya's school a good enough beating for all this drama which was to follow.

"Pass your phone." Mom said as soon as we got into the taxi. I gave her it straight away thinking that maybe her battery had run out and she just needed to use mine. "You will not be having this back until you learn how to behave yourself, you have embarrassed all of us, having the police come to the house in front of everyone, you should be ashamed". My mom was furious, the nice sweet mother act she put on for the past several hours had completely worn away, I was expecting to get beaten right there in the taxi but luckily for me mom's beating days were over. The way mom looked at me confirmed that this was the last time I can have police ever come to the house for me. She was acting as if I normally do this, police came to my house a few times, but never for me. It was always for my brother Cyrus. Mom meant business and I totally understood. I tried explaining the fight situation to her again but she was not interested, she was more hung up on the questions the police were asking and why I had answered no comment. She became just as the police officer was and began interrogating me in the taxi. I had no choice but to tell the whole truth, not the truth I told my dad, the actual truth. When I finished I awaited her response, she was on the edge of the taxi seat at the back and would not say a word to me. I knew that I had disappointed her and I felt shit for making her feel like that but I never knew that something so small would end up affecting her.

Only Uncle Jelphy was left at home when we got back, he was worried about me but Mom made sure that she told him exactly what I had told her in the car. Why would she tell my uncle if she didn't want to feel embarrassed? This did not make any sense; my Uncle had found a way to justify my behaviour, I loved him so much at that moment, finally someone that could relate to this hood life. I was starting to feel like mom did not like me anymore, all because of this fight. She sat and lectured me the whole night, reminding me of all the things I told her I wanted to be. I wasn't interested in anything she was saying to me, it all just sounded like moaning, it went in one ear and out the other, she just wasn't sounding like a mother that loved her child and I most definitely didn't love her back after the side I had seen of her today.

For weeks after, Mom would use every opportunity to bring up the fight and the fact that I was found guilty. I was so done with her! I stopped caring, I just wanted to put this crap behind me.

Me and Charlene spent our school days talking about what happened in court, we chatted so much in lessons that we were not getting any work done. The teachers would try their hardest to stop us from talking but we both had a 'don't care' attitude. Isolation never scared us, we were put in the bottom sets for Spanish due to behaviour and we were already kicked out of school at lunch times. They were running out of punishments to issue to us that we were actually bothered about. School became a chore, every morning for that week I was dragging myself out of bed, going into school late, and some days not even returning after lunch time, I just spent the afternoons going on bus journeys. I never thought about the implications that this had for my mom because I wasn't bothered about anyone but me. Come on, I had to toughen up, court was just around the corner, could I possibly face going to jail over this fight? Who knows! I just know that I had to mentally prepare for the worst which in this case was the prison sentence.

My attitude towards school was starting to take its toll on me, my behaviour became even worse; all my friends were kicked out and it was just me and Charlene left. There was no way that I was going to last for the next three months with the teachers not standing for any bad behaviour anymore. Why they thought to do this now, at the very end was beyond me.

It was a Wednesday afternoon and there was only three months to go before I left school. Time was moving so slow and I was ready to explore my new life in college. I was having a really shit day, I felt awful and I really never wanted to be at school. I found myself searching for the little voice in my head in hope that she would find me something bad to do that would issue me a reason to go home or even to isolation. For some reason, she was not showing up, at the time that I needed her the most. I ran my fingers on the wall of the corridors whilst I strolled to the head teacher's office to prove that I was in school and that it wasn't a case of truancy. Some days I was late to school but because I never reported it to the office, the school liaison teacher would call home to my mom and report it as a case of truancy. I got to the door and I could hear the headteacher shouting at a pupil. Mrs Brown was the worst headteacher ever, similar to Miss Trunchbull from Matilda only she never hit us. All day, every day she would shout about silly little things that no one cared about but she expects to be liked by the pupils. Her shouting never phased me much because I saw her for what she really was and knew that she would not last a day in the hood if she came to my ends. I took my time to knock the door because I was trying to listen to what she was saying to the pupil; Mrs Brown spoke with a high-pitched voice so most words she said sounded the same. I heard her telling the pupil that they are expelled from school permanently and that they could only return to take their GCSE's, that made me know that it was someone in my year group. I tried peering over the badly covered glass that was on the door to get a closer look because I was curious to know who it was, just as I held on to the ledge of the glass the door had burst open.

"Charlene, are you kidding me?" I couldn't believe my eyes. Charlene came out smiling in true bad girl style. She had her shirt button slightly opened, her hair was in a messy bun and just below her trousers were her Nike trainers. Just the look alone was enough to get her expelled. I asked her what happened. She had told me that it was nothing serious and that all the teachers were out to get us. I found Charlene to be really funny, her tone of voice and sarcasm was making me laugh so much that Mrs Brown was automatically angry with me.

Yes! This was good for me as I knew that it wouldn't be hard for me to get sent home. All I had to do was add a little heat to the fire and it would become an explosion. I did just that! With the help of Charlene, I started to taunt Mrs Brown "Are you out to get us Miss?" I asked, knowing full well that this was going to wind her up. Her cheeks began to go red as she tried her hardest to compose herself with silence. "Why are you out to get us Miss?" I poked and poked, repeating the question over and over again. Charlene added her two pence in by saying "YES" after each question I asked, and before I knew it Mrs Brown had blown. Typical Mrs Brown. She started shouting all the usual stuff about how we would amount to nothing and that we should be disappointed with ourselves and that we would never be anything more than fast food servants. I noticed Miss marching over to the phone and I knew immediately that she was about to contact my mom. Usually at this point I wold apologise and start to be good, however, I had no care in the world. Mom was already disappointed in me so this wouldn't have made things any worse. I walked out with Charlene and we stayed at the bus stop until school was finished. I later realised when I got home in the evening that I was expelled from school also and could only return to take my exams. I never realised the major effect that this would have had on me and my future.

Six months later and I was back at school with my friends collecting my GCSE results. I was really anxious about what they would be when that little voice in my head showed up to say what she had to say. "Don't worry, if you fail, you can always turn to drug dealing or benefits." This was not what I needed to be hearing at this point. I had an array of negative messages flowing back to me. I could hear all the bad things that the teachers had to say about me over the past five years. I could hear the disappointment in Mom's voice when I had the police show up for me but could also hear the pressure of her telling me I had to do well at school. I could hear all the other people that told me that I would not do well in life. The thing that was very strange; is that I could hear Miss Moore's voice telling me that I could be anything that I wanted to be but for some reason I did not pay much attention to that, I focused more on the negative messages I was getting because they were more prominent.

I could see my friend April across the hall at the desk with her envelope in her hand. I would envy April at school, not in a bad way but she did not have to try hard to get good grades and I always felt that I had to work 10 times harder than her just to achieve a grade that she could, without even revising for it. I used to get very depressed about students like April, I felt that life was always fairer to them and that I picked the short straw as I never had the ability to just know stuff the way that they did.

"Hey April, what grades did you get?" I asked knowing that she was going to tell me she had straight A's for every subject.

"I done terrible Seph, but I didn't really revise because of the baby" she replied. April was the second girl I knew to have a baby in school. She had her beautiful baby girl when we were in our last year.

"Well, what's terrible?" I asked, assuming that if she done terrible I may as well have walked away because life was over for me now.

"I passed everything but, I got two A's, three B's and ten C's" April said, sounding unsatisfied with her result. I swallowed a big gulp of saliva before congratulating her on her amazing results, that was my dream result, I could not believe she said she'd done bad. In my eye's, someone like me couldn't get much better than that. I got excited for her in hope to distance my anxiety for when it was my turn to open my envelope. I stood with Charlene and we linked arms before walking to the desk together. Charlene gave me a prep talk to let me know that we were in this together, we planned to celebrate no matter the result but planned a bigger celebration for if we failed as that's what we were expecting.

"Single file ladies" Mrs brown was in my view speaking again, what a b**ch, I knew that she had shown up for the grand finale of our failure. We had just come to collect results and she was on to us already. I could tell that she was just as eager as me to find out what I had got. I was not about to give her the satisfaction of knowing. When the teacher gave me my envelope, I checked that it was my name that was on there and then walked off. That cow was not having the last laugh, she would have to find out some other way what I had got and I definitely did not want her to see me upset about my result. Hally and Paris had just joined the queue to collect their result.

"What did you get Seph?" Paris asked whilst looking at the envelope in my hand.

"I don't know, it's not open yet. I will wait for you to get yours" I said to Paris, trying to lengthen the time to open them.

I waited for Paris and Hally and all four of us headed to the playground to open our results. We all became silent as we ripped through the paper, I peered around at everyone just so that I could be the last one to open mine. With a big sigh, I pulled out my results...

Pass, pass, pass, pass... the list continued with many passes, I was feeling like this was a dream. I checked again to see if it was really my name at the top of the paper, Sephuine Morgan, it read. I carried on reading the list and then I came across two fails, this was sounding more like it had to be my result. The two fails were showing against Religious studies and Spanish! No surprise there, it was the two lessons where I gave the teachers grief. I took out the other sheets so that I knew the exact grades that I had and I could not believe my eyes. "Yes, we made it" the voice in my head was aligned with how I was actually feeling. I could see A* grades, B grades and C grades. I had passed 14 out of 16 GCSE's. I was feeling so happy; the feeling of accomplishment was flowing in abundance and I could not stop smiling. I hadn't felt this feeling ever before and I knew that I wanted to feel it again. I began jumping up and down so my friends knew that I was pleased with my result. I asked my friends what they got but did not stay tuned to listen to the answer, I was zoned out and in my own little world.

It payed off!

When Miss Moore found out that I was expelled, she contacted my mom and sent her methods in which I should revise and stay focused. I had another teacher, Miss Baddams, who was my sociology teacher that was the next best thing to Miss Moore. She too sent my mom lots of work, mock papers and positive messages that would keep me engaged in my learning whilst I was kicked out of school. Both teachers done this in secret and of course risked their jobs to help me, so I had previously made a promise to myself that I would do my very best. I revised for 12 weeks straight, doing a mock paper every other day until I knew the questions off my head. I stayed up late, I stuck sticky notes around my room, I spent money on books and read them and I worked my ass off. When I was actually doing my exams and no one else knew what I was thinking, I was focussed on passing, failing was not an option for me. I had worked too hard to not answer the questions correctly, I told myself that the exams were easy and I concentrated on the key points of the questions.

But when I turned up to pick up my results, I saw all the people that were expecting me to fail and that brought doubt in my head that I was actually going to fail. I was wishing that I had opened it in front of Mrs Brown, maybe this would have made her believe more in kids like me. I had to find April, she would have been so proud of my result, I ran straight back towards the hall and April was on her way out, I started hugging her and jumping around in circles, she joined in and began jumping also, she must have figured out that I done really well in my exams.

All the girls were shouting and dancing so I knew that my

friends had passed as well. It was celebration time. I couldn't believe that this had happened. I was set up to fail and I succeeded. I kept thinking of how proud my mom and dad were going to be with my results, they always used to tell me that I was smart but I just thought they were being nice because I was their kid.

My phone began to vibrate and it was Skipper calling me. He told me that him and Jay were outside waiting for me. Me and Tanya were the youngest of the clique so we were the only ones left in school whilst the rest of the clique went to college. I was finally going to be joining the college trend. Skipper would always tell me that I was the smartest girl he had ever met and that I could become anything that I imagined. They were going to be so proud to know that I had passed so many exams and with such good grades. This meant that I would be accepted into any college of my choice.

I skipped down the school path knowing that I never had to come back to that place but I suddenly became emotional, as much as I used to say I hated school and did not want to be there, a part of me was sad to be leaving. Then I started thinking about Miss Moore and Miss Baddams, they had literally set me up on a path to success by just believing in me, no one had really done anything so kind for me like that before, I had to thank them. I was feeling overwhelmed when I saw Skipper and Jay standing at the top of the school gate. I ran to them with speed and excitement.

"I passed my flipping exams guys." I shouted, oozing with excitement.

"Calm down Seph." Jay laughed. "Well done for passing though, I always told you that you were smart."

I couldn't handle the compliments and acknowledgments. Why were people seeing me as this smart, successful, goal driven girl? I was just doing simple stuff, I wasn't smart in my eyes, I just revised and I wasn't goal driven, I just knew that I wanted to be the best and highest position social worker because it paid well and I knew that money was what I wanted. They're just being nice. My mood was set, I was absolutely happy and I was not going to let anything change that. After sending out 20 different text messages to family and friends to tell them that I had passed my exams it was finally time to celebrate, but what was there to do?

Skipper told me that he had a surprise for me but that I had to walk to the bus stop to collect it. I loved surprises so I could not wait to see what he had for me. I walked in true gangster style, still feeling amazed at my results. When I arrived at the bus stop, Rico and Ryan were there also. I was so pleased to know that they had all come down to support me with my results. I asked Skipper where my surprise was when a bag of self-raising flour was hurled at me. Were these guys for flipping real? An egg and flour fight, right here, right now, on the day that I am celebrating my achievements. I was too happy to get upset. I flung my head in my hands so that the rest of the flour didn't go all over me. My face was covered, I started shouting as if I was the hulk, put my results paper in my bag because I was not about to get them dirty and went up to the shops with the girls to get some eggs and flour.

I looked back and saw that Charlene had been covered in eggs. The guys were laughing at us. Egg and flour fights were common at school, we would have them every term without fail and sometimes twice or three times a term. The shop assistants on our school road would be so angry that the streets were left in a bad way but always served us the contents to fight. I suppose they were just money hungry folks.

I paid for two bags of flour and stole the eggs and water. It was game on, I was about to get these guys back, clique or no clique, it was girls Vs boys. Cars were beeping their horns because we were running in and out of the roads to escape being hit, random street civilians were being hit with eggs and flour, it was fun and I couldn't stop laughing. Ryan had always taken the game to far and brought extra contents such as tomato ketchup, beans, hot sauce, vinegar and all types of crap. He had squirted stuff in my hair and all over my brand-new Nike coat. Mom told me that I wasn't allowed to wear that coat to school but I never listened and now my coat was ruined. I was trying so hard to get Ryan back but he would use his strength to his advantage by holding my arms so that it was impossible for me to throw anything.

The game continued and we were playing for over an hour. The local residents were threatening to call the police and no buses were stopping for us as we all looked too dirty to even get on the buses. I ran out into the road to escape Rico when a black tinted BMW slammed the brakes on. I screamed because the car was so close and I genuinely thought that I was about to be hit. Everything around me stopped, including me. I was petrified. But I knew I wasn't about to die because the only thing that flashed before my eyes was the actual car, I never saw any traces of my life. The car horn started to beep repetitively which informed me that the driver was angered. I couldn't see the drivers because the windows were so dark but the car looked familiar.

"What the heck you doing?" A loud voice shouted from the BMW. "Get in the car!" It was my brother Cyrus and his friend Ricky. Cyrus was fuming, he started shouting at me and telling me that I could have been killed by the car and that I was being irresponsible. My friends were scattered around Bearwood high street, all covered in mess. I could only see Paris and Ryan. I told them that it was my big brother and I had to go. When Cyrus talked I had to listen. I sat in the back of his car in silence, I thought that I would give him some time to cool off and then tell him about my results which would make him forget about how irresponsible I was being.

(Meet Cyrus: My older brother, who fell victim to the hood. He grew up around Gang culture and was highly respected in the neighbourhood. Although he had enemies on the streets, he was a family man and always put us first).

I assumed that Cyrus was going to drop me home but he brought me on his errands. I was covered in smelly stuff, I could feel that the ketchup had gone down my trousers and into my underwear, I just wanted to get home and have a shower. I asked my brother to bring me home, he told me that I had to learn the hard way and that he would bring me home when he was ready.

We pulled up outside of some flats in an area that I was unfamiliar with and this crazy homeless looking man approached the car. He was itching and walking back and forth at a fast pace. He popped his head in the car window at Ricky's side and put something in Ricky's hand. I was trying to act like I didn't know what was going on but I had seen this too many times in the hood. I had seen nitty's (drug addicts) before, I pulled out my phone to look like I was distracted when I heard; "you alright luv?" This crackhead was speaking to me. I did not even respond, this was none of my business. I managed to glimpse what Ricky had passed to him, it was a white small peanut sized thing but I couldn't tell what drug it was. The man quickly walked off and Cyrus started driving. Ricky turned to give me the £20 that the man had just given him and asked me to put it in the bag that was on the seat next to me at the back. I opened the bag and it was filled with money. This was no surprise to me as my brother usually got me to count his money and put it in rubber bands for him every Friday. We had not reached 5 minutes from the shabby flats and we were making our way back to them. The same guy came over to the car, I never understood why he didn't just get all that he wanted at one time instead of wasting our time, I just wanted to get out of these smelly clothes.

Being my usual inquisitive self, I asked Ricky what he had given the man. I knew that it was not weed as I couldn't smell the marijuana aroma. Cyrus looked around at me as if I was crazy, I knew then that I had no business asking them questions, Ricky just laughed. Whatever it was I just knew that it wasn't cheap. This man had spent £40 in the space of 7 minutes, judging how he looked, you would have thought he would have spent the money on food, clothes or a place to shower and brush his teeth. But £40, I just knew that I would love making that kind of money for 7 minutes of work. I put my hand out for the other £20 to add to the bag of money. I felt like I was part of the team.

"Yo, do you lot need me to count this money for you?" I said, intrigued to know how much was in the bag.

"NO, we do not!" Shouted Cyrus.

"This life isn't all what it seems to be you know Seph, don't make that one sale fool you." Ricky said as he started with his 'father lecture'. "You see all that money in the bag?" Ricky asked. I nodded to show that I was not in the mood to hear what he had to say, but he continued with "I had to work hard for it, it never came easy, it took hard work, dedication and heart, plus with every sale there's a risk."

"Whatever." The little voice in my head emerged and said. What risk? Of course, there was no risk, my brother hadn't been to prison since he started making all of this money. Surely if there was a risk, it was really low, my thoughts began to wonder. I wanted and needed to know more, maybe I could help out some way to start earning some money, maybe this could be my new profession, I mean, it paid more than being a social worker and was a lot easier. Cyrus could see that I was deep in thought.

"Don't start getting no funny ideas sis, you should be at home, but seems as though you want to act a fool after school, I'm making you stay in them wet and dirty clothes for as long as possible." Cyrus was being evil. I gave him a dirty look knowing full well that he could not see me. I looked out the window after messaging Tanya on my phone and we were nearly home. Yes, finally I could shower off and go back out to meet my friends.

I left my clothes at the top of the wash basket in hope that my mom would see them instantly and wash them, they were filthy. Desperate to have a shower, I burst in the bathroom door and began lathering my face cloth with banana flavoured soap, switched the shower on and stepped in. It took a few washes with serious scrubbing, before all the eggs and flour came off me properly, I couldn't shift the vinegar smell, it was making me heave. I had to wash my hair which I was upset about because I had washed it a few days before, but I had to be clean. I laughed to myself in the shower thinking of the egg and flour fight and still feeling overwhelmed about my GCSE results. That laughter however, quickly turned into tears of joy. For that moment, I had so much faith in myself, I was able to do something even when all the odds were against me, maybe escaping the hood was doable. I pondered on my thoughts and told myself that day, that, I was a 'Real G' aka gangster and that I would be successful in no time.

I came out the bathroom and could hear Cyrus downstairs telling mom some exaggerated story about how he rescued me from my near-death experience. How very dare he make himself sound so heroic? He must have been trying to get the world's best son award, which he was so used to getting anyway. I left him to have his moment of joy because I knew that I would soon be interfering with my well-earned GCSE results and mom would have been more interested in me. Before the silly bus fight, I was mom's favourite child and I knew it wouldn't be long before I got back to that place.

I planned my slick entry of gliding past my brother and just dropping the envelope on my mother's lap without even saying a word. It was a quick and well thought out plan.

It failed!

Mom being mom had asked "What's this rubbish you have dropped on me." And began brushing the envelope away. I did not want to speak, she could have been a normal person and just opened it. "This has your name on it Seph." I waited a few seconds vowing in my head not to break my silence, when suddenly mom had a blast from the past, "Is this letter to do with the fight?" She asked. I was not about to go down that road, I seized my plan and said with joy "You'd be happy to know that your smart daughter has passed her exams with flying colours." I smirked and left the room in an instance to dramatize the scenario. I hid behind the living room door waiting to see her facial expression when she opened the letter, instead she was looking confused. "Mom, just look at the second paper, it's easier to understand." I suggested, as I walked back into the living room. I sat down beside her to avoid any further confusion and showed her my results. As I was breaking them down to her I could see that Cyrus was listening, Grace had come downstairs to hear also. Mom had smiles of joy and Grace and Cyrus had been congratulating me telling me that they knew that I could do it. I loved feeling supported by my family, I had made them proud and that feeling was so warming that I started to execute in my head the next best way that I could do this. I told myself that I had to stop the fighting, stop the gangster act, stop walking around with a knife in the hope to use it and to stop stealing things, those were all the things that were leading me to cause moments of unhappiness for my mom; well I guess only when I got caught for it. Cyrus pulled out a £20 note and told me to buy something nice.

"20 quid, is that all your giving me from the big stash of money you and Ricky had in the car" I said, eager for more!

I became so money hungry in my last year of school that I started to try and make money in any way that I could. I sold sweets and tuck shop things at school. Me, Grace, Simone and Tanya collected the yellow pages telephone directory catalogues that were delivered free to houses and sold them back to each resident for £1. We made fake sponsorship forms and got the neighbourhood to sponsor us, I was selling my free meal at school and going without school dinners. I just wanted money and was willing to work hard for it. £20 was not going to be enough. Cyrus looked at me with that 'I'm going to beat you up for sharing my business' look as he did not want mom to know that he had so much money.

"That's all your getting!" He snapped. I knew from his tone that I shouldn't challenge him, I folded up the £20 note and stuffed it in my bra. As I left the room, I couldn't help but think about all that had happened throughout the day. Overall, I was happy!

Lesson 3:

Believe in Yourself

If you are ready to change your life, become more successful and fulfil your dreams then you have to believe that you can do it. Your journey will be filled with people that tell you that you can't and shouldn't do things that you really desire doing. You can use this for fuel to drive you closer to your dream, which is how I usually treat those types of comments. During my time at secondary school I was told by many of my teachers that I will amount to nothing, that I wouldn't do very well in my future and that I would fail. It used to really get me down but I would focus all of my energy on proving them wrong. At the time, I wasn't aware of the belief I had in myself to succeed, but I knew that I believed I could prove the teachers wrong; and that's what I did. I went through a really rough time in my last couple of months at school because the pressure was tenfold. I had teachers down my neck that had absolutely no belief in me that I would pass my GCSEs, it was a constant put off and a daily battle. I was getting into a lot of trouble so I was in my parents' bad books and I was going through a transition of having to mature because college was so near. Life was just really hard and the only thing that kept me going was the belief I had in myself.

Now, I can look back and say that now, but at the time I didn't realise. However, some of the things I used to say to myself which I always remember, were things like; "Come on Seph, you can do it, you have to survive, you are going to win, you will pass your exams". Although, at the time, I never knew if what I kept telling myself was having an effect on me, I still made sure I told myself every day. Sometimes even several times a day, on days that teachers would get into my ears.

I had two teachers in school that really believed in me, Miss Moore and Miss Baddams. I never got to thank them. Sometimes that's all it takes. Someone to see something in you that you don't even recognise in yourself, for you to start building up your self-belief. Many of us have these people around, but we choose to not listen to what they are saying to us. We tend to digest the negative information and make it stick with us whilst regurgitating the positive information. Learn to accept positive things that people are saying about you, this will do you good.

It is inevitable that you will encounter setbacks and hard times that will last for different durations and you may even lose faith in yourself. But you can turn that around, you can start to believe in yourself again starting right now at this very moment. Forget what anyone has to say about you. Start with something small and something simple that will increase your dopamine levels and enable you to feel better in any area of your life, whether it's a relationship, business, your health or even a job. What small and simple thing can you do that will change the situation you are in right now that will ensure you are progressing forward?

- Can you improve your relationship by being more affectionate, a small kiss every morning, a hug before you leave the house or saying I love you more?
- Could you try waking up 15 minutes earlier each day just to have that time to yourself, listening to something positive or reading a positive book?
- What would make you feel a bit better at your job?
- How about exercising more, going to the gym or taking on a hobby?
- How can you improve what you eat?

It only has to be something very small, a tiny commitment that is almost un-noticeable if you are doing it daily but has a massive effect over a long period of time when you do it consistently. This will create the "building up" of your momentum and will enable you to make changes in the areas that you need to. A great book written by Jeff Olson called 'The Slight Edge' speaks about the positive impact of little things you do every day, that you think don't matter but actually do. He talks about the 'compound effect' (daily discipline of doing small things consistently) and creating big successes from sticking to those things. I would recommend you purchase that book – it's an excellent read.

Task 3: The Feelings Chart

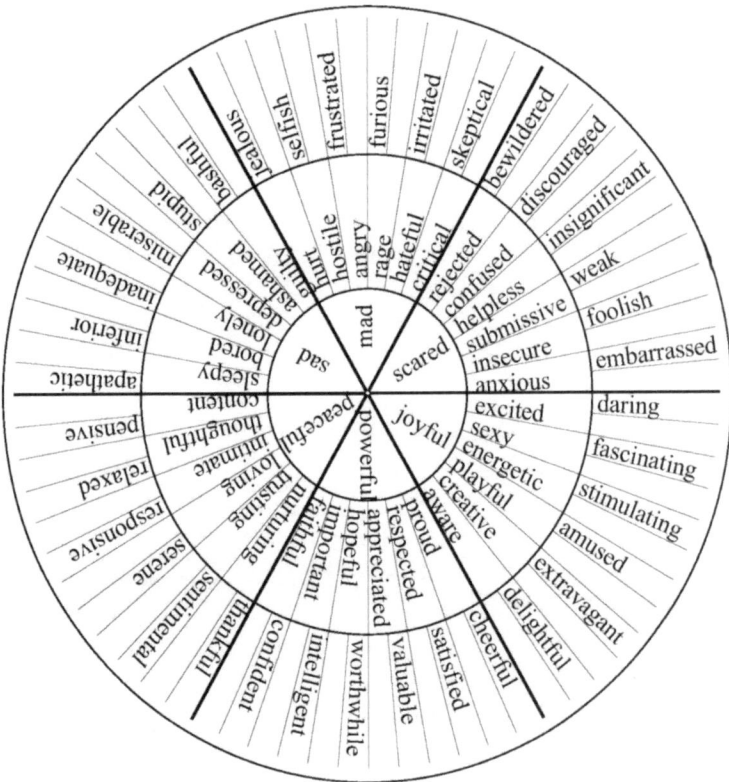

Using the chart, every day, I want you to set yourself two small daily tasks within these sections of your life;

1. Health and fitness
2. Romance
3. Bank account balance
4. Business/ Job career
5. Personal development
6. Standard household tasks (such as cleaning, cooking, washing clothes, ect)

Example:

Monday- two tasks: eat more fruit and veg (**health and fitness**), give my partner a kiss at least 3 times for the day (**Romance**), Tuesday- two tasks: Read a positive book for 20 mins (**Personal Development**), make an extra phone call to a client for your business (**Business**). However, you would have repeated Mondays task on Tuesday also making two tasks turn into four. Keep note of the two tasks that you give yourself because on Wednesday you would have accumulated six daily tasks, small but very impacting. Once you have your six tasks, you will repeat **ALL SIX TASKS** for 10 days.

I want you to select a total of 6 different colours and colour the words in the chart that best described how you felt after doing that task. Continue to do this task throughout the month until the chart is at least half coloured in, as it starts to make you more aware of your feelings. This can help you to believe in yourself because being connected to the way you feel, gives you a feeling of surety and confidence and confidence makes you believe in yourself.

Believing in yourself takes more than just setting goals and completing them. You can set goals, create 'to do lists' and achieve everything that you set out to do, but still feel like you have no self-belief. This is because you have not accepted and reflected on the wins that you have achieved. You have to get it into your system and really recognise the goals that you have conquered. Sometimes it takes someone else to recognise that, you, yourself are winning, and if that's the case then great! But when you start to recognise the wins and differences that you have achieved, you start to feel great.

Living in the hood, being around like-minded people that feel trapped in life, creates the feeling within you, that, you yourself cannot fulfil your dreams and this correlates with the type of relationships you have with people. There are some people that you can't just get rid of, maybe family members that are negative, or have a poor mindset but they are still people that are going to be around you at some point in your life. If this is the case, be careful of the energy you give to them, and what I mean by that is, yes be around them WHEN you have to but do not open up and accept the energy they feed you. Do not share exciting news with them if you know they are usually the type of person to respond negatively. Do not get emotionally connected to stories they tell you that requires you to feel sorry for them. Just be there in presence but not with emotion. I hope that makes sense to you. This is so important because one way of building your self-belief, is to not accept anything less of what you deserve. Start to tell yourself that you are significant because you are. You are very significant and the sooner you come to terms with it, the better person you will become.

What are you going to do today to better your life and walk towards your gift, talents and goals?

Remember, something small, something doable and something positive. Start today, now if you can, just by even giving yourself a few ideas of the little things you can do. Then become committed to being successful. Make it your daily do's, fit it in your daily routine. If you have decided that you want to read more books and work on your personal development, then start small. Read a few pages a day, or read for 20minutes per day. Make the time and make the effort and become so obsessed with it that it becomes habit and routine, just so much as brushing your teeth and washing your skin.

Message: You will grow through what you go through – just BELIEVE IN YOURSELF!

Chapter 4:

Shit Happens - 3 Years Later…

"I sentence you to 27 years in prison." The words kept on replaying in my head from Fridays trial, that stupid old groggy judge looked so smug when he announced it. I wanted to jump out of my seat and punch him in the face in hope that the little white wig would fall off his head and expose his true ugliness. My brother was gone and things just didn't seem real. This justice system is a fucking joke. The person who protected me since Dad decided to leave me and go 5000 miles across the world. The person who taught me how to rave in style and the person who made me laugh until I cried was just taken away from me. Yes, I knew I'd see him again but I couldn't come to terms with the fact that seeing him would not be on our terms and behind a dirty table. This only happens on TV, why is it happening to me now? The time that I need him the most. I started to lose faith in God, as he was not sticking to our plan. I made a pact with God that if I behave myself he would give me nice things and treat me well and keep all of my family safe. He failed. All the men in my life that I cared for were no longer a call away. I Just couldn't understand why he was sentenced to 27 years without proof that he had actually committed the crime. Was this allowed? I remember seeing on the news all the terrible things about children being killed and abused and the perpetrator would only get 10 years maximum. It just wasn't adding up. I knew that there was nothing I could do and I also knew that it was time to change the way I thought about life.

Cyrus was amazing to me, he had so much love to give,

everyone that was around just loved his energy. He had a way of lighting up any dull moment by telling some kind of funny joke. He was so sharp and fast with jokes that it was hard to predict when you would be a victim of his banter. I just loved every ounce of him. He would be out in the clubs and I would show up with my friends and feel super proud that my brother was the boss man in the rave. He would usually have a group of girls hanging around him with their empty glasses waiting for their free champagne. I always used to tell him that none of these women were worthy of being his wife because the extent they would go to make him notice them was undesirable. He was never too flashy with his money but it was known that he had a lot of money. I never asked my brother how he made his money, as none of that was my business but I made assumptions from all the times he would drag me around with him when he was working. It didn't matter to me, I was just happy to receive a £50 note every time I seen him in the club. This became a weekly allowance for me as I would go out every single Sunday to the towns favourite nightclub Rococo. Rococo was the place to be, even if you had work or university the next morning.

Tanya rang me to ask me if I was going to Rococo tonight. I didn't really feel in the mood as I knew that I would have a lot of people asking me about the trial and I knew that I didn't want to talk about it. I sat and pondered for a bit and told Tanya that I didn't want to come.

"Seph you're coming, it's my birthday and you cannot miss it." Tanya said.

"Tanya your birthday is not for another 15 days." I replied.

"Yeah I know but I'm celebrating tonight." Tanya sang. "Just come, if anyone asks about Cyrus I will step in and tell them that you don't want to chat to them."

We both started giggling at Tanya's much attempted patois accent whilst deciding that I was going to go out and enjoy myself. Tanya had my back and I knew that she would step in if necessary. I hung up after telling Tanya that I would be at hers for 9pm.

I met Simone and Tanya at their house for exactly 9: 00pm and we started to prepare for the night. Simone was in her dressing gown dancing around the house to Floetry's album and Tanya was in the kitchen pouring us all a cocktail.

"Talk to me Seph." Simone sat me down and told me that she knew that I was not being my usual self. I felt as though Simone was my earth guardian angel, I used to hear old people at funerals or at nanna's house talk about being protected by a spirit which they called their guardian angel. I could resonate because Simone was exactly that person, only she was alive and there in the flesh. Simone could always pick up on my energy when I wasn't feeling good, I don't know how she done it. I was smiling and acting as if I was ok but deep down I was thinking about my brother and was hoping that he would be ok. Just as I was about to tell her that I am ok, she looked directly in my eyes and I couldn't stop the tears from rolling down my face. I knew she could see my true feelings, I burst out crying. Simone sat in silence hugging me listening to me trying to get the words out, I don't even know what I was saying, I just felt really emotional and felt that I had to let it out. It seemed as though I was crying for ages and I was ready to go and get dressed for a good night at Rococo. Simone hadn't said a single word until I finished crying, she then released me and held my hand

"Girl, I can tell you've been crying and you need somebody to talk to, I'm your girl, you're my girl, were all girls..." Simone was singing the Destiny's Child hit single and dancing around on the chair.

"Shut up Simone." I giggled pulling my hands out of her palms. I could not believe that she was making a joke out of the situation. We laughed and started to get ready for the night. Suddenly my cocktail sprung to mind, I darted for my drink in order to change my mood. I did not want to go out and change the pleasant vibes that both Simone and Tanya were sharing. It was time to liven up.

On the kitchen side were bottles of coconut rum, ginger wine and a variety of Asda juices. My glass was already filled but I felt it was necessary to add a double shot of coconut rum to shorten my journey to 'tipsy land'. Before you know it, I was feeling slightly more in the mood and we were ready to leave. "Tanya you're driving." Simone shouted as she was putting on her last heel to leave the house, Tanya was upstairs taking forever to get ready when she shouted back; "No, I can't drive, it's my birthday." We all laughed, eventually making our way to the club.

Just as we pulled up we seen the ignorant bouncer that always acted a fool. After seeing us every weekend, he still proceeded to give us trouble on the door. "Can I see some ID girls?" He said. "No! you flipping fool, you have seen it the past 52 weeks. You should know our flipping ages off by heart," the little voice in my head said, nearly making me repeat it. "Yes sir. Here's my ID," was what came out instead, in the most sarcastic patronising voice. I kept a smile on my face as this bouncer's behaviour was unpredictable and I was not about to get sent home and walk the carpet of embarrassment past the long queue of people who were waiting to come inside.

We got in the club and as usual everything was going great, people were dancing and having fun. I decided that I was going to be getting drunk today just so that I could drown my sorrows and not think about my brother, so we went straight to the bar to get drinks. The cocktail that I had previously had went straight through me, I never even felt moved. I ordered two whole pitchers of sex on the beach and told the bartender that I did not need a glass as I was going to drink it from the jug using the straws. I meant business! I started straight away with no hesitation, Tanya and Simone told me to slow down and pace myself but the nerves were building up because I could see my brother's friends. I literally had 35 seconds to get as drunk as I could, so I drank and I drank until the 1st one was finished. We hadn't even found a table or space to dance and my brothers best friend Ricky approached me with a hug. I felt from his warm tight hug that everything was going to be ok, Ricky was good looking so that made my hug so much better, he told me that I didn't have to talk about anything and that he will give me anything I needed. I knew that Ricky had been in touch with Cyrus because they were very close and Ricky seemed as upset as me in court on Friday as if he had lost his right-hand man. He ushered us over to the rest of my brother's friends and took my drink off me to put on the tables they had. Ricky headed towards the toilet in a hurry, I giggled as I thought he was on the brink of urinating in his True Religion jeans until I seen him coming back with three bottles of Moet champagne.

"These are for you ladies." He said, placing it on the same table as my pitcher. "Yes, I'm getting drunk in this club." The little voice in my head sung. I shook my head as if it would shoo my alter ego away, I didn't feel in the mood to listen to anyone, especially not her. Tanya started pouring our drinks whilst Simone was dancing away and I started to feel much more relaxed. I could tell that Rococo was going to be good that night as DJ Silk was playing and was just about to go on the decks. Twenty minutes into his set and the party was pumping and I felt good. Suddenly, from nowhere the crowd to my right started running in the direction that we were in, this meant that some drama had started and possibly meant that someone or a group of people would be hurt. I squeezed myself behind the table pulling Simone and Tanya near me out of troubles way. It looked like two guys had a disagreement and got into a fight, there were tables being thrown, drinks and even bottles. This was a perfect opportunity for me to let off some steam but it wasn't my beef. "You better beat somebody up" the voice in my head told me as I waited for someone to accidentally fall into me. I began shaking my head even more to completely silence my inner voice before it got me into trouble, it was too late and I became anxious, with my palms starting to sweat. The feeling felt too familiar, I gathered that this was the process my body took me through before making a rational decision although I knew the outcome was always 99% bad, it felt great. At that point, I was wishing I knew someone involved just so that I could release some energy. My wish became true, I seen Ricky pick up one of the Moet bottles off the table and throw it at one of the guys that was fighting. It was time to rumble! He must of known the other guy as Ricky wasn't the type to get involved in business that was nothing to do with him. I felt that I had to get involved for my brother's sake; Ricky was practically family. I ignored the fact that I was a young girl and once again my inner gangster sparked. The bottle hit the guy in the head and his blood splattered everywhere, it was pouring down his face but he was still charging towards the guy that he was after and also Ricky too.

Change of plan, I knew immediately that I had to stay out of the way, I was not about to get blooded up. This guy was made of steel and reminded me of the robot in Terminator two (liquid man), who Arnold Schwarzenegger could not defeat for a long period of time. It was time for me to leave. This was becoming too regular, for the past couple of months there had been fights almost every week at Roccoco. This couldn't be life. I was fine when they were just fighting but to see blood pouring down that guy's head and to see Ricky involved in something so horrific just made me want more for myself. I was experiencing mixed emotions, one minute I wanted to be 'about that gangster life' and then the next minute I wanted to go home and never experience the drama again. This was two grown men, two women's son's and someone could be killed. If my mom had known about half the things I had seen going on in that club she would be at the door every Sunday night making sure I stayed in.

I stumbled from behind the table as we decided to make our way to the nearest exit through all the carnage.

No! This could not be happening now, the sex on the beach pitcher I had demolished and the three glasses of champagne had started to take a toll on me. Everything was moving in slow motion, I kept ducking down to avoid the flying bottles I seen coming towards me, apparently, they were nowhere near me but it was better to be safe than sorry. After what seemed like 40 minutes of hard battle, we made it to the club exit and I looked back to see if Ricky was ok, I knew he could handle himself but no one could keep Mr. Steel back. Ricky was nowhere to be seen and I became very anxious and worried. The police sirens started to go off and what started off as a small fight between two people ended in multiple arrests and blood everywhere. Typical hood behaviour.

It all clicked to me instantly, just like that light bulb moment you hear people speak about, I needed to be more than this. I needed to steer away from this hood life, that could have been me. I was 19 years old and the past two years had been shit. My nan passed away and it completely changed the dynamics of the family, it broke down, we went from spending every Sunday together with aunts, uncles and my cousins to seeing one another only on special occasions. Usually deaths bring people closer, but for our family we all drifted apart. It was just mom and her army of kids against the world. My dad had decided that he wanted to move to America to better his health and for better career opportunities. I took that as a selfish move because my dad meant everything to me, I was a daddy's girl and he just up and left before I even had my own house. He always used to say that he wanted to take me to America to live with him but the thought of leaving my mom, sisters and the clique was too unbearable. Besides, Dad didn't understand me anymore. Whilst I spent less weekends with him as a teenager, our connection drifted, so he no longer knew what all my favourite things were. I couldn't just leave everything behind. I started to behave even worse when he left and never really got used to the feeling of him being gone. He would contact me every day when he first moved out there, then it became less and less. I went into true rebel mode and I hated everything and everyone. The years were just getting worse and I had to do something about it.

Many girls were hurt in the fight at the club and that could have been me. I started to question why I enjoy this hood life so much, where young people are beaten up, robbed, bullied and killed. What did I enjoy so much? There was blood everywhere, it was luck that me, Simone and Tanya were not hurt tonight or even arrested and this was becoming normal. I slowly started to sober up after slapping myself in the face and telling myself to wake the hell up. "Go home Seph, this is not what you want for yourself." The voice came back but this time I didn't want to shake her away, this gangster inner me was starting to speak life into me. She hadn't been positive for the past 19 years, she just told me to get involved in a fight and now she was telling me to go home. I wondered if the old inner me had been kidnapped and replaced with a good girl. It wasn't the time to think about it, I just followed the instructions and went home.

We pulled up outside Tanya's house and I decided in that moment that I was not going into University in the morning because I knew I would be hungover. We sat outside in the car just speaking about the nights events. Tanya got a phone call from our friend Nemo who was also at Rococo, saying that when we had left, the club was shut and everyone had to leave, he said that he was making his way to come and chill with us for a while. Nemo and his boys were also great friends of ours, they were from Handsworth and we were always in Handsworth because my nan lived just off rookery road. There was Nemo, Adam and Michael, they would come around after college and hang with us and even go to youth club with us. The guys in Winson Green were sceptical when we brought new friends around, especially when they were guys. To describe it I would say, it was like two dogs first crossing paths, very unpredictable; they would give each other 'the stare' and then start barking uncontrollably to show whose territory it was or they would just pass without any trouble. For our neighbourhood, the guys were always barking mad. Thinking about it now they probably felt threatened that their girls would be taken away. They were the guys we hung out with as little kids and now they had to share us, I get why they would feel like that. They took to the clique very well, in fact they had no choice, the clique became our brothers really quickly, we bonded in a way that we never did with the neighbourhood boys.

Nemo showed up with Adam and Michael, they opened Tanya's car door and we all began speaking about the craziness that had happened at Rococo. I was still in a daze and thinking about why my inner thoughts were starting to look out for me rather than get me into trouble. I had so much on my head, my brother being the main thing, the fight that had just happened and I was feeling stuck in a situation that I couldn't change. I kept trying to visualise what life would be like in April's shoes. April was my only school friend that was different to me, she had everything, her dad was rich, her house was huge and extraordinary, she always had money at school, the latest phone, some crazy gadget and she would get top grades without even having to revise. I stayed in contact with April, I was so inspired by her life that I tried to imagine myself living in a house like hers and living life having everything that I wanted. I was in a blur for what seemed like a long time and I just knew that life had to change no matter what it took.

I noticed Skipper had arrived also from Rococo. He came to the car to see if I was ok. I was sat at the back on my own whilst Simone and Tanya were in the front and Nemo and his boys were standing, leaning on the opened front driver and passenger doors. Skipper could see that I wasn't ok but said that we will talk about it tomorrow. We all got out the car and was chilling on the street all dressed up. At that moment, I was so thankful that I had amazing friends that could get me to smile after such a terrible weekend.

I had noticed a guy from our area walking down the street towards his house, his name was Shaun; he thought he was a total hard nock and the godfather of the area, but he never gave any of my friends or me any trouble because he was scared of my brother. He was slowing down as he approached us and had never seen Nemo, Adam and Michael before. What was he doing? I mean he wasn't about to hang out with us, I know that for sure; Shaun had a hi and bye relationship with us and would sometimes say more when he was asking about our new friends. He began staring at Nemo in an uncomfortable manner, Nemo was much younger than him, but Shaun was out numbered.

"Lord please don't let anything bad happen". I found myself turning to faith again after deciding earlier on that I had given up on God. The little voice in my head, for the second time in one night tried to be on the positive side of life. Shaun continued staring, causing an awkward silence and uncomfortable energy.

"You alright?" Nemo asked, breaking the silence.

"Yeh, I'm all right." Shaun replied in an aggressive tone.

Why oh why, I began wondering – should Nemo have not opened his mouth? Or should Shaun have a bit more respect for the general public. After all he did not even know who these guys were, they could have been sons of the greatest Mafia or even members of the Notorious gangs of Birmingham. Shaun walked through us and kept turning around to continue his awkward stare that he had started. What an absolute prick, I knew I was safe, I wanted to use that to the advantage and say something to him but my words were held back, it must have been the discovery of the new me. I started not to like this new me and wanted the rowdy me back just for this moment, how dare he just try and intimidate us like that for no reason?

We all watched as Shaun walked on home, he had already looked back two times, I was hoping if he done it again he would bang right into the lamppost that was near him just for the inconvenience of trying to intimidate us. He looked back again, Nemo had enough and said "What's the problem?" Whilst raising both arms. I don't know what part of that offended Shaun but he had acted as though Nemo had shouted the most offensive thing in the world. He came marching back up towards our direction and I could see everyone around me getting prepared for a fight, even the girls. We were about to beat him up together if he had tried to get physical. I knew Shaun could fight, hence why he thought he was the neighbourhood's Godfather but we weren't about to go down like that. He was ranting and raving, shouting "do you know who I am?" and kept repeating it. Well duh! Of course, they don't know who you are. Shaun was seriously angered and the situation was starting to spiral downwards. I had a flash back of the fight that had just happened at Rococo but this time I imagined Shaun to be the one with blood pouring from his head. Yes, my inner gangster was coming back and I needed it if we were about to beat up Shaun.

Someone from the area had heard the commotion and came out to defuse the situation. Unfortunately, he was younger than us all but somehow managed to get Shaun to go home. "Phew, that could have got messy." Simone said as we all laughed in shock of the situation that had just occurred. We started to discuss all the things we would have done if he became physical.

Then, all of a sudden, there was Shaun marching right back up to us again. This time he had his hands in the crotch area of his pants. Was I the only one seeing this? Maybe it was deja vu. I looked at everyone's face and realised that this was really happening. When someone in the area had their hands in their pants, it usually signified that they were carrying a gun and you were expected to run. No one moved! I knew we couldn't dodge bullets but something didn't add up in this situation.

It made no sense at all, there was no beef. You wouldn't shoot someone for asking what the problem was from a stare that you forced upon them. The simple maths was not adding up. Shaun got about 5 feet away from us and pulled out the gun. It was an all-black 9mm handgun and had the word 'RUGER' written in silver. He began shouting aggressively and waving the gun at us. The young guy from the area tried to calm him down but it was not working. He then began pointing the gun at us individually, we were crazy to even speak back in the situation, but I heard everyone saying "what do you think you're doing?" I saw him approaching me and thought that he would have skipped me if he knew what was best for him. But something must have taken over him that night because he was looking directly in my eyes and saying some crazy stuff that I couldn't make out, when he had put the gun right in my face. At that moment there was no fearful emotion, I was so blown back by what was happening that I could not feel anything. I was completely numb. My reaction took me back, I began swearing and saying some crazy things to him, he must have forgotten who my brother was. A gun! Now that's the worst thing he could have done, he may as well have shot me because it was just as bad. I then started feeling mixed emotions, what if he killed somebody. The gun pointing went on for about 3 whole minutes and it was all one big, loud catastrophe. I could see neighbours at their windows peering out, it's like everyone had heard except for Simone and Tanya's parents, how could they not hear and we were so close to the house. None of the neighbours bothered to get involved, they would have looked out and seen that it was not their kids and closed back their curtains. Again, the young guy managed to pull Shaun away and take the gun out of his hand, he and Shaun ran off towards the direction he came from.

What the hell had just happened? We were all left angered, we quickly became the victims of something so stupid for no reason.

Was this karmas way of telling me to calm down and stop trying to feed this inner gangster, or was this my queue to turn it up a notch and by myself a gun for protection? I had no idea and couldn't fathom what had just happened. Me, Simone and Tanya felt bad for having brought the guys around such a foolish person and put their lives at risk. We kept on apologising. They were accepting and told us that it was not our fault. Something had to be done, Shaun could not get away with that. For a second I had forgot where my brother was and took out my phone to call him. Ricky sprung to mind as he was the next best thing. I called Ricky about three times but his phone kept on going to answering machine. I gathered that he may have been arrested from the fight. I sent him a message;

"Call me Ricky, its IMPORTANT!"

Ricky got back to me around 40 minutes later but by then I was laying on Tanya's bed about to fall asleep. He told me that he had just spoken to my brother and they had to sort some things out. I told Ricky what had happened, he was so shocked and asked me a bunch of questions about Shaun. I felt like he was the police, I was under pressure to tell the story a few times over and to describe Shaun to him. This was just the way that Ricky done things, he was so used to being in a gang from the age of 11, to now being 33, he knew exactly what he was doing. Ricky had been to prison four times before and was currently on a class A drug charge which he was due to go to court for soon. He told me that everything would be ok and that he will have a word with Shaun.

The next morning, I woke up to the sounds of police sirens. It was a new week and the same crap was happening. Things that were normal for my neighbourhood were starting to irritate me, I was feeling more and more trapped in the hood. I started to feel that I would be better off going into university even though I had planned not to, because going in meant that I was one-day closer to becoming an IRO and having a professional job and getting away from all this mess. I had work later that evening also, I worked in the book makers as a cashier whilst studying because I loved having money and knowing that I had made it for myself and no longer relying on my mom's funding was always a great feeling. I was also saving up to fulfil my dream and move away from the hood. One of the things Tanya's mom Sharon told me is that it is really important to save whilst I live at home with my mom, because when I leave I would have to fend for myself and by saving it would enable me to have extra little things. She always went on about how expensive being an adult was, but I never really understood. I took her advice and saved, I never touched much of my student loan money and that was the biggest lumpsum that would fall into my bank account. I remember applying late for student loan on purpose, which meant that I was back dated by two months, I received a payment just short of £4000 and I felt that it was enough to call myself rich.

I packed my bag for university and got into my car to drive there. When I looked in my back mirror I seen that Shaun's house had two police cars and tape around the house. Maybe someone secretly called the police on him to report the gun. I knew that none of us had called the police because we weren't allowed to snitch, whatever happened in the hood stayed in the hood. I then thought of Ricky; did he kill Shaun? I never knew what Ricky would do I just knew that he would go to any measure to protect me, and with Shaun pulling a gun on me, he basically threatened my life. The feeling of wanting to go to university went away again. I took my phone out to tell my friends that I wouldn't be coming in again and made my way home. Mom was cooking and my little sister Sophie was just leaving to go to school. My mom had done her usual run to the shop in the morning and had bumped into Shaun's mom. She began telling me that Shaun was home last night when some guys broke into his house by shooting the keyhole off and put a gun to his head. I couldn't believe what Mom was saying to me, the smirk on my face was apparent that I was enjoying what she was telling me, I just kept on saying "he deserves it" mom kept on telling me to "be nice", but she had no idea what I was about to tell her happened last night. She then said that before the guys left Shaun's house, they shot his dog. I'd like to think that was his personal warning, or even karma. Both suit me just fine.

The story was getting better for me, he had hopefully gone through what we did last night, all the mixed emotions and wondering if we were going to die or not. I was worried for his dog. I began telling mom about the night before.

"Mom grab your tea, you're going to need to sit down for this one."

Lesson 4:

Survival

Growing up in a disadvantaged area, or even being the black sheep of your family can make you feel as though you are fighting, just to survive. You feel yourself running on your own energy in hope that it is enough to keep up with survival. Survival is so important, not just in the physical state but most importantly the mental state. You have to be a survivor in your mind.

Declare to yourself now that you are a survivor. I want you to say the words out loud.

I AM A SURVIVOR... and when you are saying it, don't just read it but affirm it, make it sink in and picture yourself being in survival mode. (I usually picture myself as a hungry lion that has to feed the cubs, I spot my prey and I succeed- it gets quite graphic, but it works for me).

Having been brought up in such a poor and ghetto area, the way I used to think about life was distorted. I have had friends murdered, locked up, shot, stabbed and even take their own lives, all being victims of the hood. Sometimes you hear things on the radio and in the news and just think "this wouldn't happen in my area" it almost seems surreal and you think the media have completely made it up from scratch. Well that's how it was for me but for people that were portrayed through the media as successful. I would read an article and see '18year old just made 1million from technology invention' or 'young person earns their Bachelor Degree from Harvard University' and 'young entrepreneur sets up their business at the age of 15'. I would see the article titles and think that it was a completely surreal story, fake and made up for monetary purposes. That is because as a poor community, we only knew how to survive literally, we never knew the meaning of survival through business, survival through opportunity. We literally just knew how to make ends meet for us to eat and have a home…and that was just some of us.

My vision of life was distorted and survival for many of us meant, going out and not getting killed. Survival meant sacrificing a bill to have food and survival meant all the family staying in one room in winter because there was not enough money to pay gas to have the whole house heated up.

Now the reason I share some of these things is to notify you that, it was within those moments that created an urge for me to do better, want more and to grow strong enough to survive. There is no doubt that the best survivors have been through the worst struggles. As I mentioned previously, you don't know, what you don't know. So, at the time, my childhood was great. But in reflection, I realise all the things that I never had, opposed to what I could have had growing up as a child. Everyone will experience this, that's why when we have our own children, we say things like "I want for them what I never had" or "I want better for them". We can all relate.

In the chapter above, I speak about the incarceration of my brother, who I always refer to as being a survivor. If you have found that you have ended up in a situation that is out of your control and in this situation, it was prison, then you also have to have your survival instinct intact in order to get through the sentence. This can be applied to many different situations, through business, through relationships and through life's strongest storms. You just have to be strong.

Survival is about fighting through, not just gliding through. You have to create the opportunities you want, you have to fight for jobs that you want to stay in, you have to keep on coming back every time you're told no. Life is going to constantly test you on your ability to survive through the toughest storm. Are you ready to be a survivor? Yes!

Message: Only the strongest survive.

Chapter 5:

Choices or Consequences?

Ricky and I had become really close, he took on Cyrus's role and started looking after me as his younger sister. I kept on telling him the story of what my mom heard about Shaun in hope that he would tell me what happened. But he just kept saying that "Karma has the most important job to fulfil." As well as, telling me that it was none of my business. I never pushed for any answers, Shaun had seen me a few weeks after the incident and apologised for what he did. Maybe he was on drugs that night, or maybe he had some point to prove. Whatever it was, he made the wrong choice. I did however, feel like I no longer had to worry about Shaun. That was all done and dusted and life could go back to normal.

I had gone to pick Ricky up from his flat as he told me that he needed me to drop him somewhere. This was fine, I didn't mind driving him anywhere he asked, as he done so much for me, this was the least that I could do for him and I knew that I would leave with a full tank of petrol. I arrived outside Ricky's flat and called him to let him know I was outside. When he came down he had a huge rucksack on his back and was swinging a large plastic bag. He opened my boot and put the bags in. When he got in the car he asked me how work was, I was telling him that it was fine and that I had been saving a lot of my work money so I felt rich. He then started asking me more and more questions about my rate of pay and concluded that I was worth so much more than £7 per hour.

"What do you want to be when your older Seph?" He asked.

I am older, I thought to myself, I was nearly 21 and felt like I was a big woman. "I'm at University studying Social Work and hope to become an Independent Reviewing Officer, someone at the top of the ladder." I replied to Ricky.

"And what do they earn?" Ricky asked, sarcastically.

"55 Thousand a year, big money," I said with joy thinking about the life that I would have when I started earning that money.

"Open your mind Seph, that is not a lot of money – how do you expect to become a millionaire on that wage?" Ricky was passionate, he was trying to make me think of something that I had never thought of before. I was not used to people talking to me like this, I assumed I had it all planned out, I knew exactly what I wanted to be. That should have been enough, it was better than what most people knew in the hood.

I never thought about what Ricky was asking before, I just knew that £55k a year would change my way of living and that's what I wanted; to escape the hood. After drilling me with all the reasons why I am worth so much more money, it suddenly surfaced that he was right! I was worth more than £7 per hour. However, I had no way of even knowing how much more I was worth. Maybe Ricky had all the answers.

"How much do you think I should be earning then Rick?" I asked in hope that he would spark my mind to think of a better figure than £8 which was only £1 more than what I earned.

"There's opportunities out here sis and if you can't see any, you have to create them. I shouldn't be telling you what to earn, you should know how much you are worth. Why do you think I have all this money, all these cars and my clothes? I know my worth and the lifestyle that I deserve, I work hard and people pay me what I am worth. It is as simple as that!"

Ricky had me thinking about my future. I needed to be even more than an IRO. What could I possibly be though? The little voice in my head appeared "You can just about be an IRO, why are you trying to push to be more?" The little voice always decided to show up when I didn't want to hear her. I was confused, it took me years to think of what I wanted to be. Ricky had just changed my mind in an instant. He lived a good life though, if he was telling me something like that, it was because he wanted me to experience a better life.

We carried on with the journey and Ricky could see that I was deep in thought about everything we had spoken about. He told me not to worry and that he would look after me whilst Cyrus was away. "We are family and family look out for each other." I knew that Ricky would never betray my brother, he was like family and had been around since I can remember. After a long-awaited pause of silence, Ricky spoke; "Work for me Seph, leave that silly job you are at, I can make you loads of money and you know I will look after you."

"Work for you?" I was unsure of what Ricky actually even done as a job and now he was talking as if he had as business.

"Work for you doing what?" I said with a cheeky voice.

"I will have loads of jobs for you to do, but you can start off by being my taxi and driving," he said casually.

"Driving? Driving where and how much do I get paid?" I asked. The inquisitiveness was present, as much as I thought Ricky was joking, for the fact that he may be serious, I had to know what my pay was because it would reflect what he thought I was worth.

"I'll pay you whatever you want, just pull over here." He pointed out the street to where he was going and then got out of the car. As he walked to the boot to take the bags out, a middle aged looking guy, small and chubby with fair skin and dark hair was coming from the office that we were outside of. He was wearing a dark grey tailored suit with a crisp white, perfectly ironed shirt. His tie was a deep purple and his shoes looked as though they had just been polished. He greeted Ricky with a hand shake whilst taking the bags off him, tapped him on the back and ushered him inside the office. I kept an eye on Ricky as I thought that the man looked really strange, in a way that, he wasn't the type of guy that Ricky would associate with. In fact, he looked like a member of the corporate world or even an undercover policeman. He was suited and booted and looked like he knew nothing about the streets much less the struggle.

Ricky came out after 5 minutes and had a big smile on his face.

He was holding a food container that was sealed with cling film and had his rucksack on his back. He walked over to the boot, opened it to put the bag in and then he came back in the car with the food container.

"You hungry Seph? You can have this," he said as he pushed the container on to me.

"I don't want that. I don't know where that has come from and if the police looking man you were just with, made it, I definitely don't want it." We both laughed and started making our way back to Ricky's place. When we arrived, Ricky handed me some money. I couldn't tell how much it was because it was wrapped in elastic bands.

"What is this for?" I asked, curious to know why he had handed me bundles of money.

"That's your first pay, three bills," he said.

"£300. What have I done to deserve this?" I asked him, astonished with the amount he gave me. At my job, I would have to work a whole two weeks to make that kind of money. I was only with Ricky for an hour.

He replied, "I pay good Seph, and I told you to open your mind about making money. It's time you leave that job. I spoke with Cyrus and he's cool with you working for me. Hand your notice in ASAP. It's time to take your mind and your money to the next level." I couldn't believe that Ricky had just given me so much money, I wanted in! I wanted to work for him every single day. "I could leave my job with this rate of pay." The excitement was oozing from my body as I was putting the money in my purse. This was easy work, all I had to do was drive Ricky places, just as a taxi would and I would be paid for it, not no chump change, but real cash. "Same time tomorrow?" I shouted out the window laughing as Ricky left the car. He waved me goodbye and told me to call him if I needed anything. I danced to every tune playing in my car all the way home before meeting up with Ryan.

Dinner was about to be on me, I was loaded for the day. I would never walk around with £300 cash in my purse, so I thought, I may as well spend it…easy come…easy go. After all, I was back at work tomorrow.

I met with Ryan outside my house and hopped in his car to go and get some food. As soon as I jumped in the car I noticed that Ryan was eating a bag of sweets. "Where we going then" he asked whilst chewing on his sweets.

"Are you not going to offer me a sweet?" I said, holding my hand out waiting for my share of the sweets. "Let's go somewhere fancy, dinners on me." I sneered. Ryan looked at me instantly and began to giggle.

"I am being serious Ryan, let's go somewhere different, a bit up market, somewhere posh." I reverted to my serious tone so that he knew I was not joking.

"Ok fine, I know this place that does really nice Chinese food, it's not a buffet, you order off the menu and the staff are great" Ryan said.

Ryan knew all the best places to eat out so I was confident that the restaurant was going to be tasty. I still couldn't clear my mind of how much money I had earned and in such little time. This was madness! I knew that Ryan could sense the excitement that was going through my body, it was obvious to anyone. I kept moving around and I was just full of happy gas. I had to tell Ryan exactly how I made it. I began telling him everything in intricate detail. I knew that anything I shared with the clique would stay with us, we were family and the trust we had in each other was strong. I was going on and on, not missing a single detail when Ryan stopped me and asked "what was in the bag?"

"I don't know, I never seen" I said. I was not even bothered about the bags contents, I just made £300 in one hour with no risk. It was smooth running's.

I wasn't about to get my mind thinking about what was in the bag because I didn't want anything putting me off from doing it again. "Seph, just be careful" Ryan said, sounding worried about what I had just done. Ryan was very hard working and worked in the car trading field, buying and selling cars. He worked long hours and really appreciated and knew what he wanted out of life. He was one of those 'always look on the bright side' kind of people that seen the positive in everything. I knew that he was just looking out for me and wanted me to gain the most from life that I could. Everyone needed a friend like Ryan just to keep them seeing things in a better light.

We sat down in the posh restaurant and had a look through the menus, I had no idea what to order as when I had Chinese at home I would get the £1.60 combination that was chips, curry sauce and rice. If I was lucky our family would have a chow mein and some chicken wings, but Chinese in our household was most definitely a luxury. Ryan ended up ordering a bunch of things that looked and smelt so good, I couldn't wait to get stuck in. We conversated about many things whilst eating, the food was delicious. If this was what being wealthy tasted like, I wanted to be wealthy. I thought the Chinese we ordered at home was nice, this was much more divine. The waiter came with the bill and complimentary drinks and sweets. The bill came up to £100, this would have normally shocked me, but I had just made £300 in sixty minutes, believe me, I had it to give. I pulled my purse out to pay when Ryan, put his money in the waiter's hand and shooed him away.

"I am paying Ryan!" I shouted, annoyed that I never had a chance to pay. Ryan told me not to worry about it and got up ready to leave. Every time we went out to eat, Ryan would get the bill, no matter how much it was. I just wanted to return the favour, Maybe next time!

On the way back home, I received a message from Ricky that read:

"Work @ 9am 2mo, gonna be longa than today."

I replied: "Yeh kool."

I failed to realise at the time that I had work tomorrow, at my normal job. It was easy to calculate a decision about where I wanted to be…with Ricky. But how was I going to get out of work! Tomorrow was going to be the day that I handed in my notice. I wasn't scared about leaving my job because it was only a temporary post whilst I crept up the social work ladder and had nothing to do with social work, I was just a cashier and thought that I could have got another job easily if all never went to plan.

I woke up the next morning thinking about what Ryan had asked me. What was in the bag? I wasn't stupid, but I didn't want to make any assumptions. I thought it was cannabis as everyone in the hood smoked Cannabis and I never really classed that as a drug as such. I decided that when I met with Ricky, I would ask him.

I called in sick to work and left out to go to work with Ricky. Ricky was already outside waiting for me when I got there.

"You're late Seph," he said getting into my car.

"Ricky, it is 9: 03am I am only three minutes late," I said. That wasn't late to me!

"The main thing I need you to do, is be on time, if I tell you that you start work at 9: 00am, then try your hardest to be here from 8: 55am. Punctuality is important for anything that you do in life." He said.

I sighed as I was not in the mood for a lecture, Ricky was always teaching me something about life, something valuable that I could use when I became older. "OK Rick." I said, hoping to shut him up. He put the destination in the satnav and we were ready to go. This time Ricky had no bags with him, maybe we were rolling with nothing today. It sparked in my mind that I should be asking what was in the bag yesterday, so with no hesitation I asked away;

"Rick, what was in those big bags you had yesterday?"

"Drugs were in the bag Seph." He replied so casually without batting an eyelid.

My eyes opened widely and promptly with my head tilting slightly back. "Drugs? What type of drugs?" I must have sounded shocked by the expression that Ricky looked at me with.

"Crack and Heroin." Ricky was not holding back any information, he was telling me everything. Now was the best time to find out everything I needed to know. Maybe even mention Shaun, to see if Ricky would confess to shooting his dog.

"Well why are you telling me everything?" I asked, still astonished by his answers.

"Because you asked, and I would rather have you know exactly what you're going to be dealing with at work," he said.

I had nothing to say, I was literally speechless. Ricky's honesty was throwing me off. I stayed quiet for what seemed like a long time just thinking about if I wanted to be around drug dealing first hand. In the hood it was normal to hustle. You could be selling weed, selling stolen goods, selling something but I had never been in this situation before. I didn't know if it was for me, but I was loving the money so much that I hadn't had time to think about any of the repercussions.

Ricky got out the car when we stopped. Today was different from yesterday, he told me to turn off my engine and come inside. As nervous as I was, I went, because I knew that Ricky would not let anything bad happen to me. We stood in front of a tall block of flats and he pressed the buzzer. He stood in silence before someone buzzed us in, without saying hello. That made me know they were expecting Ricky. When we got in, we went to the fourth floor and inside the door on the left. I could hear noise coming from inside the flat. I knew that there were a few people present but I had no idea who they were. I had never been to this place before.

The door opened and the guy behind the door looked like the walking dead. He smelt so bad and had dirty ripped clothes on. This must have been one of Ricky's customers surely. The guy told us to come inside and then shut the door behind us. I held my breath and kept releasing it for little five second breaks to make sure I did not inhale too much of the stench. I couldn't describe the smell, it was a new scent that I had never encountered before but I hated it. Ricky shook his hands, I cringed and my body froze as I thought that the man was going to want to shake my hand. I diverted my eye contact and looked around so that I seemed less friendly, I was not about to be my usual 'people-person self' because I didn't want to touch him. We followed him through to his living room, walking over empty coke and 7-up cans that were left on the floor in the landing area. My feet were coming out of my trainers with every step as they stuck to the sticky floor.

The living room looked like it had been ram-sacked, it was very busy. There was no way that people actually lived here, there was no space for them to live! Every step you took was a constant dodge of something on the floor. Ricky was obviously used to it because he glided over everything without paying any mind to it. There were things all over the place. Boxes were piled on top of one another as well as stacked up, against the walls. The Tv was resting on an old wooden school chair with mounted paper keeping one of the legs steady. Papers and unopened letters were scattered across the floor, there was clothes on the kitchen counter. The nicest thing they had was a glass coffee table placed in the middle of the room. I couldn't help but notice the white powder lines that were perfectly straight and small cut out pieces of cardboard, along with cigarettes, weed and medical syringes. What the fuck was this house that Ricky had me in, surely Cyrus wouldn't want me to see all of this. "They must be living with rats." The little voice in my head appeared, I agreed, she was right, this is what a rat's home must look like.

Strangely, one side of the kitchen counters was completely clean. It stuck out like a sore thumb and kept on deterring where I was looking. They obviously used that side of the kitchen for something important.

The man that opened the door for us wouldn't keep still, there wasn't much room to move around but he made space and kept walking around the room. All of this strange behaviour was normal to Ricky, he never batted an eyelid. He began taking some sealed packages from underneath the green battered sofa that was missing a cushion from one of the sides. He took his pen knife out and cut the package open. The man came over to Ricky, dipped his finger in the package and licked it off. He then put his thumbs up and continued to pace up and down the room.

"Sit down Jack, your scaring my little sister." Ricky said to the man. "She's not your sister!" The man blurted out whilst moving around the sofa deciding which side he was going to sit on. I was not scared of him, I don't know why Ricky thought that, I wasn't scared of anyone. I did however think that his behaviour was very strange. Anyone would, he wouldn't calm his ass down, what was I to think?

(Meet Jack: A drug addict that lived in the hood. Jack had many opportunities but chooses to live in the way that he does because of his addiction. Jack has been to rehab many times but never ever completed the programmes).

I was sure that I heard other people in the house because it sounded loud when we approached the door. But Jack was the only person that was present. I thought about sending Tanya the emergency message. (The emergency message is a call for help that would get you out of any situation you are in). I would have made Tanya call me and act like I needed to leave and then go, but I couldn't leave Ricky on the job with no driver. So, I stayed put!

The back-room door opened and out came a tall slim woman, she was so beautiful and looked really young. She had jet black curly hair and a huge smile with perfect white teeth. Her dimples sunk right into her face when she smiled and she had big brown eyes that resembled marbles. She was wearing a fur beige jumper that hung off her right shoulder and black leggings. Her toenails were painted in a bright red to match her finger nails and she was stunning. She was the complete opposite to smelly Jack (which later became his name) that had just let us in. I heard Ricky call her Sonia when he said hello, so I assumed that was her name. Sonia, greeted both me and Ricky and was about to offer us a drink.

"NO thank you." I said quickly before she could finish asking us. Ricky, said yes and waited for his drink to be made. My stomach churned at that fact that he would be drinking from such a messy house, with a horrible smell. This was against everything Ricky stood for, surely.

I had to stay in the living room with Jack whilst Ricky and Sonia went into the other room to talk. Jack had waited for them to leave the room then started sniffing the lines of powder up his nose through rolled paper that resembled a straw. I felt so uncomfortable just watching, I didn't know where to look when I heard Jack whisper. "Do you want some?"

"No flipping way you freak," I replied. Jack laughed his head off. I wasn't laughing, but he sure found it funny.

"Your brother would kill me if I gave you some." He said as he continued to chuckle.

"My brother would kill you if he knew you were sniffing coke in front of me, and so would Ricky." I said, hoping that this would stop him taking the drugs. Jack didn't care, he was moving so fast and kept his eye on the room door that Ricky went into. I knew from the way he was acting that he didn't want Ricky to know what he was doing. He looked at me with a straight face and then gave me a huge smile. I knew that the drugs had, had an immediate effect.

After sniffing up all the lines from the table, Jack sat on the cushion less side of the green sofa and picked up a small glass lightbulb looking thing that had a tube coming from the side of it. I never knew what this was until he lit it and started to smoke it – a flipping crack pipe.

"Hey that's enough now, you tryna kill us?" I asked him. But he was so out of his head that he did not even acknowledge that I had spoken to him. "Where was Ricky? Why did he not let me wait in my car?" Were the thoughts that kept on circling in my head. I tried to make some sounds that would attract Ricky's attention, I started clearing my throat loudly but I could hear them both continuing to talk. I had never been around someone smoking crack before, how the hell am I supposed to act? I held my breath, I wasn't trying to take any breaks for air anymore like before, I feared that if I inhaled the smoke that I would become a crack addict and I was not going to take that risk.

I could hear Ricky and Sonia speaking in the next room, but I was trying to make out like I was watching the tv and minding my own business. They were speaking business, I could hear them talking about locations and prices, where the drugs were going and how much money they will make. I was gobsmacked, the figures were sounding unreal. I continued to hold my breath until it became uncomfortable. I think I inhaled a whiff of the crack smoke because I felt sick. It smelt like lots of different random things were just burning. I then quickly held my breath again. Jack looked over at me when he heard me gasp for air, I think he thought that Ricky was coming back into the room. He jumped and started to pack the things he was using away. I already made my mind up, I was going to tell Ricky anyway, so I don't know why he was trying to hide it, plus the smell was revolting.

When Ricky came back into the room, Jack was wiping his face up, the little punk had put fresh lines on the table so it looked like he never took the ones that he did. Ricky stared at him for a long time. It's like Jack had an on and off switch. He began acting normal, well what was normal for him. Ricky never clocked onto anything, he just gave me the signal to leave, he was carrying a huge bag, that must have been filled with drugs, well that's what I thought. We left the flat and went back to the car. Thank God, I was out of that crack house, I don't know how Sonia lived with Jack being as clean and beautiful as she appeared.

I was telling Ricky about my terrorising experience of being in the same room as a drug user. I told him everything that Jack done and even mentioned to him that Jack had offered me some cocaine to sniff. Ricky got angry and said that he could not believe that Jack had waited for him to leave the room. Ricky apologised and said that it would never happen again and that he will sort out Jack. I was interested to know about Jack and Sonia's relationship to Ricky and what that flat was all about.

Ricky told me that the flat belonged to Jack and that Jack held a very special place in his heart. He spoke about the flat being used for business, that's where they had their drugs delivered and that is where they broke it down into packages for sale. It all made sense, no neighbours would suspect that this drug addict was running a drug operation in his house, because they would assume that he would tempted to use all the drugs. However, this wasn't the case. Ricky trusted Jack, and Jack had respect for Ricky, so everything that they were doing was running smoothly. I was so intrigued but that was no excuse for Jack to be a smelly mess and it never explained Sonia's role. I sensed some sort of chemistry between Sonia and Ricky so I asked him if they had history. He said they were once an item but became very good business partners. "Yeh whatever" that does not happen in the real world, I thought.

"Sonia has a very good heart Seph, in life you will meet people that you know you should not let out of your life forever. She is one of them people." Ricky said.

"Yeh right, you fancy her and that's it" I said as I tried taunting him about liking her.

"She's a good business partner to have, she knows the ropes and she's been around me and your brother since we were kids. Plus, she does a bloody good job with looking after my brother. He would have been dead by now if it wasn't for her." Ricky gazed out the window whilst he was talking to me.

"What brother Rick? That's news to me, you have never mentioned your brother. Who is he, how old is he and can I meet him?" I asked. Ricky never ever spoke about having a brother nor did Cyrus mention it. Maybe he was a long-lost brother. As far as I could remember, Ricky was the only one. When I would go to his mom's house, there were pictures on the wall of just her and Ricky, no one else. Ricky's phone began to ring and he told the person that we were nearly there.

Ricky asked me to pull up outside the launderette, our conversation was over and I had no idea what we were doing here. Maybe the owner of the laundrette was an undercover drug dealer and used his laundrette business as a cover up. Ricky took the bag out of the car and brought it inside, he then opened it and tipped it upside down. A bunch of clothes fell out on the floor and I saw Ricky give the man some money.

We went to the laundrette to wash clothes! I was confused, all of this was cutting into my valuable work time. I thought we were supposed to be on the streets like real drug dealers. I missed work for this?

I was moaning to myself in my head as I never wanted to sound ungrateful saying it out loud but what was he doing bringing us to the laundrette when I am sure we had more important things to do. I was getting paid either way so I should have just relaxed.

Ricky came back out and sat in the car, he seemed exhausted even though we hadn't done much, he kept going through his phone and shaking his head, something must have been on his mind. I wanted to finish off our earlier conversation but it wasn't the right time. I asked him if everything was ok, he brushed it off as if it were and we continued with our day.

As the day went on, I started to be exposed to more things; drug houses, where people would literally be cooking the drugs on a stove, drug addicts and drama. It had only been a few hours and I felt like I had seen the lot. I was overwhelmed with everything that I had seen and I knew that I had enough for one day. I started to question whether this was worth the money after all. I didn't know anymore, I just knew that I was not going to leave my job, I was going to stay on track and become what I wanted to be – an IRO.

It was 6pm and I felt really tired after all the driving around that I had done, I filled my tank again for the second time in a few hours. I was ready for bed, but work had not finished. We made several stops at Jack's flat whenever Ricky needed to reload his stash and we spent the day meeting people, some of whom we saw a few times in that day. Some of them had just finished their 'corporate world' jobs. We met women, couples, business men people that did not look like drug users, we met the lot. I mean where the hell was all their money coming from? Some looked like they couldn't afford a home much less drugs, but they always paid. People in the hood were poor and these people were just out here flogging their cash on a fix, something that made them feel good for a few hours. This was crazy. This couldn't be life for these people.

I never ended up handing in my notice at the bookies because I got into a routine where I could fit everything in. I spent the whole winter working for Ricky and making a lot of money. I spent so much money over the months on takeaways, clothes, alcohol and things that I never even needed and all because I could. The money was so easy, easy come and easy go. I never saved much which was strange for me because all the time I got my monthly pay from my job, of like £600 I would save half and then slowly spend the next half and a chunk of that would go on my car insurance and petrol. It's strange how your mind works, I was so used to making quick money, that I never saw the point in saving it because I never thought it would stop.

I didn't ever think about the implications that this lifestyle may have had because everything was so well planned, the police was the least of my worries. What we did never appeared risky, things just ran so smooth. Until one day I was trying to get through to Ricky for work and all the numbers that I had for him were out of reach. I decided after a few hours that I would go to his house and see if he was ok. I was worried, Ricky was about the gang life and me not hearing from him could only have meant two things. 1: He was in the police station or 2: In the hospital! The possibilities were scaring me. I raced to his house and went right to his door. When I got there, I seen that the door was covered in wooden planks.

The Police!

They had Ricky, a part of me felt at rest because I knew he wasn't dead but then I started thinking that I would be next on the list. If they have Ricky, surely, they would be coming for me next. I was just working with him for the past several months. What was I going to do? Ryan and Tanya were the only people that knew I done a few jobs for Ricky. I even played it down to them because I knew they would tell me to stop. I was doomed!

I went home and stayed in bed for the whole day waiting by the phone to see if my brother or Ricky would call. I couldn't function properly; the day was going super slow. I sat and waited for hours and then... Cyrus called.

"Hey sis, you ok?" He said, greeting me as he normally did when he rang.

"No, I'm not ok, it's all messed up. The feds have got Ricky, they kicked off his door and now all his phones are off," he could tell from my tone that I was worried. "What's gonna happen to me bro? Mom can't find out anything." I said nervously.

"Leave it with me." He said.

"Hello," I could hear my echo in the phone. Cyrus had hung up. This was not what I needed right now, I needed reassurance to know that everything was going to be ok.

Five minutes later and my phone rang again.

"Sis, it's all sorted your fine, just live your life as normal and don't worry about anything, no one is coming for you." Cyrus said.

As much as I wanted to believe him, I just couldn't rest. Were the choices I made to make fast money about to ruin my whole life?

I told myself that night that I would never do anything like that again.

The next morning, I received a text message off a number that I wasn't familiar with and it said call me when you can.

I didn't want to take the risk, immediately I thought it was the police trying to trick me and catch me out. Maybe they got my number from Ricky's phone and they were trying to get all his acquaintances. I ignored the message and continued with my day. The same number started to ring me about 45 minutes later. I answered the phone but didn't say anything.

"Hello." I could hear that it was a man on the phone. It was definitely the police, I was not about to speak to them so I left the phone running, in hope that they would hang up.

"Hello, flipping ell, this girl... HELLLOOOO," the man said and started to giggle.

It suddenly clicked to me...It was Jack, that laugh was tailored to him.

"Jack, is that you?" I asked.

"Of course, its flipping me, you ok?" He answered.

"Yeh fine, have you heard from Ricky?" I sat waiting for him to say yes.

"Of course, I've heard from him, he just rang me. He's doing great, the coppers have got him in Winson Green Prison. He will be there until his court date" Jack said.

"Ok. Do you think he'll buss case?" I asked.

"We flipping hope so, don't we kid?" Jack began to chuckle again.

He found everything funny, this was a serious matter but he managed to find the humour in it.

"Has Ricky asked for me, will I be ok? I was asking Jack loads of questions. I just wanted to speak to Ricky directly, that would have made me feel better.

"He told me to ring you because he knew you would be worried. Everything's ok, you have nothing to worry about. If you need anything you're going to have to ask me." Jack said.

"Ha ha ha, very funny Jack!" I replied. Jack wasn't laughing this time. He couldn't help me, he needed help himself but here he was offering a hand. Joker!

"I mean, if you need any money then I can give you some, right kid, I've got to dash. Save my number, it may come in handy." Jack quickly put the phone down. He was so weird even when he tried to be normal.

It was over! Just like that, all the money I was making was put to an end. I couldn't help but think about Ricky's supporting customers, what would they do without Ricky's services? These people relied on him to be available every single day. I knew that I wasn't going to be making anymore fast money, but Ricky would have been hit hard. He was losing thousands per day.

Months later, Ricky's trial came up and he ended up getting sentenced for 5years. I had spoken to him a few times and he reassured me that things were going to be ok. He apologised for not being here for me as he promised and told me to stay on the right track. Get my education and keep on living my dream, legally. He told me that if he got sentenced he would need a few favours off me, "Nothing naughty." He would say. I trusted Ricky and told him that, I will help him however I can. He wrote me a letter and he asked if I could keep an eye on his brother because he would normally get Sonia to do it but she was going away for a few months because she needed a break and needed to stay low. Sonia was deep into the drug game and had to get away, in case the police was on to her.

I remember Ricky saying that his brother was older than him, I was younger than Ricky, how was I going to look after his older brother? I didn't feel I was capable of doing that. Maybe he had some type of disability and just needed a carer. Ricky sent me the address of his brother's home and said that I would need to go there and meet his mom. He also told me that his mom would show me what I need to do, to help out.

I couldn't say no, Ricky had done so much for me when he was out and I knew that he wasn't going to make me have anything to do with drugs ever again.

It was a Saturday afternoon and I had been making countless

amounts of excuses every time I was supposed to go and check on Rick's brother. I just did not want to be taking on the responsibility of looking after anyone. But, today I decided that I may as well. I mean, I didn't have anything better to do. Life had become so much slower once I stopped operating the drugs phone. I called Rick's mom to tell her that I would be making my way over there. She was so happy to hear from me, I hadn't spoken to her as much now that Rick was away, she told me to come around for 4: 00pm as she was tidying up.

I left from Winson Green, following the satnav, that had taken me on the Aston expressway to Erdington. I was 5 minutes from my destination when I arrived at the gates of a beautiful home. It had a large path that you had to drive up, before even seeing the house. When you got to the top of the drive, you were greeted by two large black shiny gates that only opened once you spoke to the operator.

"Welcome to the Mando residency." A posh voice said through the microphone. I put my windows down and popped my head out as if I were ordering something from McDonalds. "Sorry sir, I think I have the wrong house," I said whilst double checking my phone and satnav to see if I had entered the correct address.

"Turn around Seph, this is the wrong place." The little voice in my head muttered.

Without any hesitation, I put my car into reverse and began to wind my window up.

"Sephuine Morgan, is that you?" The posh voice said again. How does he know my name? It must be Ricky's brother, I thought, before answering;

"Yes, it's me, is Dawn there please?"

"Yes, come on in. Dawn is awaiting your arrival".

I watched as the gates began to slowly open. The driveway was big enough to fit six cars on it and the grass surrounding the house was beautifully mowed and a perfect green. The house stood tall and looked like three houses were joint together. It had large Victorian windows and a beautiful archway over the door. Wow! I could not believe this is where Ricky's brother lived. This was a dream house. No wonder why Ricky had high expectations of what he wanted out of life. It dawned on me that someone living in such a beautiful place needed to be looked after by someone like me. Surely there was enough money to hire somebody professional.

I couldn't wait to get inside to see what the rest was like. When I got out the car, I fixed my clothes and made my way to the door. The doorbell was so loud and sounded old school, like something you would see in a movie. The door opened, and in front of me stood Jack!

Jack!

"Are you kidding me, what the hell are you doing here?" Jack and I had a love/hate relationship. Some days I would greet him with a clip around the ear and other days I wouldn't say anything more than hello as he would be too high off his face to even recognise who I was.

Jack had made an effort today, he scrubbed up well. None of his clothes were ripped. I mean, he still looked a bit dirty and his hair was really scruffy but he looked much better compared to how he usually looked.

"Mom, Seph's here," he said in a youthful tone. Why was Jack calling his mom, I was supposed to be meeting Ricky's mom, to be briefed on how to look after his older brother. "Mom!" I said, looking at Jack confused. "Is your mom here as well?" I asked him. This couldn't be what I thought it was. There was just no way.

Jack began doing what he done best, he laughed and laughed, for no reason at all. He was such a weirdo most of the time. I don't know if he was always like this growing up but I knew that the drugs were having a major impact on his personality. Ricky always talked about how great of a guy Jack 'used' to be, but he never spoke of him in the light of it being his brother. I was standing in front of Jack, watching him laugh when suddenly everything Ricky had said in the past about Jack was coming back to me.

I started to ponder on the things I was told about Jack.

No!

It doesn't make any sense!

I should have pieced this together a long time ago.

Ricky's mom Dawn came down the stairs and was making her

way over to me. I couldn't hear anyone else in the house. But surely Jack's mom was hiding somewhere.

"Hey Seph, come and give me a squeeze." She said as she grabbed me to hug her.

"Mom, you show Seph around," said Jack using the same posh voice that I had mistaken for a house-butler earlier. I looked at Jack and he had a smirk on his face.

"You're such an idiot Jack, that was you?" I felt like punching him. He was always messing around.

What the hell was going on?

It was clear.

Jack was Ricky's brother!

How was this even possible and why had Ricky been hiding Jack all these years? I couldn't wait for Ricky to call me so that I could ask him all these questions. I just couldn't understand it. Jack was a crack addict, he lived in a squalor and he smelt awful, Ricky was handsome, clean, all the women loved him and his flat in Handsworth was decorated beautifully. This did not match up.

After being confused with the shocking information, Dawn gave me a tour of the house. She could see that I was thrown by Jack calling her mom and gently tapped me on the back telling me that she will leave it up to Ricky to explain everything to me. I kept on shaking my head as we walked around, unsure of what I had just discovered. Dawn took me on a tour, it was like nothing I had seen before in my whole life. Everything was just immaculate and supersized, I didn't even want to step to hard, even the floor was delicate. It was the complete opposite to Jack's flat. How did he bare being in that rat home he called his flat when he had the choice of being in this luxurious mansion?

Whilst talking with Dawn, I got to understand that it was Ricky's house. He had brought it a few years back and had designed it in a way that was fit for a royal family. Everywhere was luxury, Ricky must have been so proud of everything that he had achieved with this house.

I was starting to understand why he would lecture me all the time, I mean if I could have a house like his, that would make all of mine and mom's dreams come true. Mom and her army of kids would have fit into this house with there still being room for any additional family that wanted to stay. And to think that Ricky has funded it all! I was blown away and instantly inspired. This is what Ricky meant when he told me to open my mind.

In the past two years, Jack's addiction had become really bad. Ricky believed that it was the hood that made him even worse. So, he decided that the best thing to do was remove the hood from Jack. He already tried removing Jack from the hood but that didn't work as he never stuck around to complete his rehabilitation programmes.

I think a part of Ricky felt guilty because he was a drug dealer and his brother; a crack addict! Ricky supplied to people like his brother and never thought for a minute that a family member would become an addict. It was crazy Karma! Ricky had spent so much time trying to keep Jack away from the drugs, but Jack only made improvements when he was away from the hood.

Dawn started teaching me everything I needed to know to look after Jack. He could pretty much do everything for himself, he just needed to be supervised at all times. I started to think back to when he snuck the cocaine lines in front of me and questioned if, I could even manage looking after him, he never respected me enough then, what's the difference now? Jack came upstairs and stood with his hand around his mom's shoulder, hugging her whilst looking at me. I rolled my eyes, "this is going to be fun Jack" I muttered sarcastically. We both stood, fake smiling at each other.

Dawn interrupted, re-assuring me that everything will be fine and that what I had to do was easy. "No trouble from you Jack," she said knowing that he was likely to give me trouble as he always wound me up. I stuck my tongue out at him as Dawn turned her head, just in time for her to see him reply with his middle finger. "Jack, no trouble I said!" She shouted before pushing him back in the direction where the stairs were.

Ricky was only a call away and still had everything under control, I was starting to feel less anxious about looking after Jack. Perhaps we needed some alone time, so that I could get to know what his personality was really like.

Making my way down the stairs, I never wanted to leave just yet, I needed to admire the home some more. Jack followed behind me, asking if I wanted something to drink. This house was beautiful and clean, I was ok to have a drink from here. "Yes please" I answered. I sat on the chair in the living room, lost in thought about Ricky and Cyrus. Until my trail of thought was disturbed by a cushion flying into my head. "Make it yourself." Jack giggled. "Urgh!" I sighed, in frustration. "You're so annoying," I shouted before getting ready to go home. I was only there for just over an hour and I had already had too much of Jack. I said my goodbyes to Dawn and left to go home.

I got emotional when I sat in my car admiring the house and thinking that Ricky was not even here to show me what he had achieved. The court system was unfair. My brother and Ricky were taken away from me and losing so much time for something so silly. This was becoming so regular around me, everyone was either getting locked up or dying.

There had to be change!

All the big ballers around me, that most of us aspired to be like, were now imprisoned. The illegal way out of the hood which I learnt throughout my childhood couldn't have been the only way out. "I'm going to be rich…legally." I told myself before setting off out the big black gates.

I decided that I would forget about all the fun I had making money with Ricky because none of it was worth it now he wasn't here, him or Cyrus. I would give it all back just to have him on the streets being a brother to me. Something has to change!

Lesson 5:

Always Follow Your Gut Instinct

Have you ever felt a feeling in your stomach that is telling you something, but you choose to ignore it? That feeling is what they call your 'gut instinct'.

Your body has a powerful relationship with your mind.

The thoughts that you transcend which feel like powerful intuitions connecting with your body and signalling you, letting you know that something is not right; that feeling of sweaty palms, or a racing heart and the millions of working little men pulling at things in your belly, that is your gut feeling! It is designed to keep you safe, prevent you from life's dangers and pre-warns you, on many occasions of what's to come in your life.

We all have an intuition. There are things we need to know, decisions that we need to make and messages that we need to pass on that come in the form of intuitive messages. Sometimes things lead us to clues, through dreams, food cravings and even strangers that tap into the inner intuition to enable we find the answer to something we want to know. Your body is a power house and you have an inner psyche, just as I do.

It is important that you trust the messages that you are receiving, especially if your heart and soul are in agreement. Your gut instinct will guide you through life and always has your best interests at heart. It is there to protect you.

In the chapter above, I talk about what typically happens throughout life and specifically in the 'hood'. We sometimes end up in situations that we know, do not serve us any purpose from the get go. But for some reason, we continue to pursue things even when we have been given the messages that tell us not to. You have to make the right choices in a society that is built against the majority, in order to grow and succeed.

Many people that I have grown up around have been trapped in this vicious cycle of life, where they; do something wrong that is financially fulfilling and because nothing bad came of it, they do it again and again until it becomes the norm. Then in most cases, it backfires on you and you are punished for it. Which can, (in the example of Ricky) lead to imprisonment and ruin your future career. Ricky became accustomed to a specific lifestyle (selling drugs) that was initially based off wrong doings.

Most people know from the beginning, when something is wrong and doesn't serve any purpose but they do it anyway to fulfil the smaller, most instant satisfaction. You must follow your gut instinct and make decisions based off what your gut is telling you is right.

I speak about the night when Ricky was arrested. Ricky had been feeling uneasy all day and couldn't put his finger on exactly what was wrong. He was later arrested on the same evening, I remember how anxious he was throughout the day, over something that he couldn't predict. I don't go into much detail in the story but on that day, he had a huge drug exchange which the police had inside information to. He was so close to not going through with it, but pursued against his gut instinct. He was arrested on that night and jailed for 5 years. Unfortunately, the jail life became a jail career for Ricky, in which he spent a further seven years away.

The choices you make are important!

Be responsible for the choices that you make, own them and make sure that they better your future and bring you one step closer to your dream, every time. We will be making choices until the day we die which will ultimately shape our future and everyday lives. This is why it is so important to make good choices that serve you well, opposed to the example used in the story.

One of my main reasons for wanting to get my book out there, was to get it into the minds and hands of people that feel like they cannot escape their issues. There is always a way out, a way to be freer, live your purpose and quite importantly, gain financial satisfaction from it – with the choices that are made. And your gut instinct is a forceful driver that can bring you to your destination, if you let it.

Listen to your body and the messages it is trying to give you. We all experience it, when something is off in our body, but we can't seem to put our finger on exactly what it is. The feeling frustrates us, so much so that we start searching for all the answers of what it may be. Everything that you are supposed to know will come back to you in some form and way.

Make good choices, good choices to better your health, good choices to make money, good choices to have a better relationship and most importantly, good choices to become a successful entrepreneur.

Message: Listen to your inner intuition – no one knows you better than you!

Chapter 6:

Everything Is Going To Plan!

It was the beginning of my last year at University. I sat in the class with my classmates, all being from different backgrounds to me and could not believe that I had made it this far. How was I here? This surely was not the path that the hood had created for me. I did not want to get ahead of myself and talk too soon and mess up, so I kept taking every day as it came and never really had the time to celebrate my journey. My lecturer had been going over our dissertation when I had an instant hood attack. The little voice in my head who I named Gemini for the obvious reason of her having severe split personality, came at full force. "You know this life is not for you! How far do you expect to go? The hood needs you, it is where you belong, people like us cannot be successful in the corporate world." An array of negative messages started to attack my soul and for that moment I felt worthless, I had decided university was no longer for me. I began getting sweaty palms, my heart beat started to race and I felt like I was going to be sick. My classmate Whitney had noticed what was happening and asked if I was ok. I did not even know how to answer the question, I just knew that I did not fit in the room and I needed to go back to the place where that voice in my head told me I belonged. I dismissed myself from the session and ran to the bathroom; the sick was coming at full force. I threw myself in the cubicle and it all came out. The bathroom was quiet so I assumed no one else was in there. I began crying, I was so emotional and did not know what was happening to me. After months of cheering me on, little Gemini just had the power to control exactly how my life would be and today she decided after two whole years, that university was not for me. Why was I wasting my time? I was giving myself all the excuses I could think of to back up the fact that the little voice in my head was correct, I had to do as she said, she knew me best, but I was battling with myself. I wanted to go to university, this was a plan I had ever since I was a little girl, I had borrowed so much money to pay for my course and my family and friends were super proud, I couldn't quit now. I stared at myself in the mirror and looking back at me was someone I did not know, the person in the mirror was a university student, not far from obtaining a Bachelor Honour Degree. I no longer knew myself, I just took each day as it came, showed up to class when I needed to and did everything that my lecturer Mr. Potter had told me to.

(Meet Mr. Potter: Mr Potter was my university lecturer who had a massive belief that I could become anything I aspired to. I assumed he had come from a similar background, with a poor family and never did too well at university himself somehow but was now teaching young adults to become successful.)

I heard the toilet flush as I was looking in the mirror at myself crying, another girl was in the cubicle. I tried wiping my eyes fast to deter any attention. She looked up at me and smiled whilst fixing her jumper and rolling up her sleeves to wash her hands. I tried keeping my head down and making myself invisible but it never worked. The girl started to talk to me. She asked me what I studied and how long I had left. I was not in the mood to be answering her but I couldn't be rude to her for no reason - she was smiling with joy and appeared to be so happy, it would have been horrible for me to put her in the mood that I was in. I started to answer her after clearing my throat. When I told her what I studying and that it was my last year, she had said how happy she was to have met someone in their last year, who just so happened to be studying the same thing she was.

She began asking me lots of questions about what she should expect for her last year, I could feel the sick re-surfacing but tried my best to keep it down whilst speaking with her. It was like talking to a younger me, she seemed to be taking a lot from what I was saying to her. I could tell that she was excited and grateful because by the end of our conversation she kept on thanking me. I couldn't understand why, it was just a conversation, in fact, I had only answered all the questions she had asked me. I didn't ask her anything about herself because I wasn't interested. I didn't even want to be speaking with anyone. She left the bathroom and said "Everything happens for a reason – I was supposed to meet you today." She was holding on to the door and staring at me as she was saying it, I thought she was weird, I was starting to feel a little freaked out. Was she really there or was that a guardian angel? That stare had shaken me up. I opened back the door after she left to check that she was a real human and there she was walking back towards the classroom area speaking with a guy. The words she said had startled me but it made me feel good to know that I had helped her in some way. Maybe I should stick university out! A lot was going on in my mind and I didn't know what I wanted.

Suddenly I became emotional again, I cried even more. What an absolute wuss! I had no idea why I was crying, I felt sad and angry. I was battling with myself. I looked at myself in the mirror again, this time looking directly into my own eyes and began saying "I am great, I am amazing, I am going to make it through university, I am going to be successful". It was something Simone had told me to practice doing when I felt sad or down as a way to pick myself back up. I looked and sounded pathetic! This wasn't for me, it must not work on me, I didn't feel any better.

I tried it again, "I am great! I am amazing! I am going to make it through university! I am going to be successful!" The tears were coming faster and I felt like I was going to be sick again. What the hell was happening to me? I am not a 'sick' type of person, why am I vomiting, crying, and feeling so strange? It was time for me to go home; my mind was made up. "Well done Seph, great move," Gemini appeared with her snide comments. I decided, I had made the right decision. I was quitting university!

I drove home in my brand new Peugeot 207 convertible. It was a shiny, black with sports seats, very clean and smelt so good from the cherry car freshener that I always used to buy. I had decided to treat myself with a new car after having about £15,000 in my account. I became obsessed with saving money and saved up most of my university money as well as working my ass off, all year. I would have had nearly double that money if I continued to work with Ricky – my thoughts started to wonder. Every day I was thinking about Cyrus and Ricky, all the wasted time that they had exchanged with the law, missing out on family events, and most importantly for Cyrus, missing out on his daughter's childhood. All of a sudden, all that money they made couldn't change the situation at hand.

Ricky helped me to understand money in a different way and it made me passionate about making as much cash as I could. Luckily for me, the friends I surround myself with, were the same. All we wanted to do was make money and go on holidays. So we did!

My holiday visit list was being ticked off rapidly. I travelled to many different places with my girls and the clique. Malia, in Crete, was my favourite place to go. Partying and enjoying life with all the money that I had made myself. I became solely dependent on me and the feeling was great, now I really understood what Ricky was trying to teach me.

In fact, Mom noticed that I was earning a bit of money and to top that off, I was great at keeping it, so she said that I had to start paying my way to get myself prepared for when I leave home. This didn't bother me as I always wanted to be able to help my mom out.

I started to buy little things for the house that I had visioned myself living in. My room at home had become full of household items, an iron and iron board, cutlery, bed sheets, kitchen utensils, plates, cleaning products, the lot. I thought that I needed to move in to my new place and make myself at home straight away.

I pulled up at home and took my phone out, I had a message from Whitney asking where I was, I told her that I went home because I was feeling sick. I wasn't lying, I felt sick as well as feeling like a low life. I couldn't tell her that I decided to quit university and that I have a voice in my head that decides what's best for my life. She would think that I was absolutely crazy. Mom was home, getting ready to go to work, I could never really show my mom my emotions if I was crying because she would go into defence mode and want to find the person that made me cry. If anyone of us cried, it was usually someone's fault in my mom's eyes. That's all she knew, after being in a abusive relationship for over 15 years. When she cried, it was because her monstrous partner made her cry, so she thought no different with us.

I tried looking as normal as I could but she could tell from my voice that something was wrong. I made out like nothing was wrong and went to my room, throwing myself on the bed with my head in my hands.

Mom had to leave for work so I was going to be home alone. At that point I felt like I wanted to just run into her arms and tell her exactly how I was feeling but I didn't want to stir up any disappointment because I knew how proud she was that I was going to University. Grace had moved out to go to university in London and my little brother and sister were at school, I had no one to moan to. I wasn't used to being alone in silence, in such a hectic house. Someone was usually always at home. Today that someone was me and I wasn't feeling it.

That sudden movement of throwing myself on the bed made me feel sick again. I ran to the bathroom and let it all out. Something wasn't right! I'm never this sick. I tried remembering what I had eaten throughout the day to track if I could have had food poisoning. Then realised I only had two pieces of toast, which I struggled to eat.

Could I be…? No way! I checked my monthly cycle calendar in my phone.

I was late… by 5 weeks!

5 weeks, what the hell had I been playing at not realising that I was late?

I called Tanya straight away, she was at university also but I managed to get her at a good time. She answered;

"Hello."

"Tanya, I think I am pregnant," I whispered as if someone other than us both was present.

"What?"

"Yep you heard right, I keep being sick and I am 5weeks late."

The tears began again. I told Tanya that I am done with university and that I had enough with striving to become successful in a place where I did not fit in.

Tanya would usually be in agreement with me as we always thought the same about things but instead she had asked me if I was crazy. She said that she was leaving university to come and take me to the clinic to get a pregnancy test. I needed my best friend at that point so badly. She was the only person who would have kept me sane, so, I was grateful that she said she would drop her plans to come with me.

Tanya was outside in an instant and we drove straight to the clinic to get a pregnancy test. I started telling her all the negative things that Gemini had said to me to make me leave university and told her why I was quitting. Tanya told me that I was not leaving until I got my degree and that we had come too far to just give it up. I had a think about what she was saying but it did not overpower the fact that I felt like I would not be accepted in the corporate world and reach my full potential because of the upbringing I had and area I was from. I didn't want to be the tea lady in a big corporation, I wanted to be the manger, I wanted to be in the big chair and make the decisions but my mind was telling me that I should get a normal job like everyone else in the area and stop trying to be someone who I was not.

"Miss Morgan." The nurse from the room that I had just given my urine sample to, had called me back to give me the results.

"The result has come back positive." She said, in a calm and happy tone. I could not believe what the lady had just said to me. I asked her to explain what she meant.

"You're pregnant, you're having a baby, you are 9 weeks gone and in your first trimester." She continued talking but it all became a blur, I just remember her saying folic acid, and eat healthy. This explained the sickness that had come from nowhere. I had to tell my boyfriend!

I left the room and told Tanya that I am going to be a mother.

Tanya was smiling and hugging me, it sounded so strange to me. Me? A mother. Wow! I rang my partner and told him the news, he sounded happy, which gave me a sense of relief as I knew that our decision was made and I was about to become a mother; but I wasn't prepared! I had learnt from college and university that things always work out better when you plan and prepare. I was not prepared to be a mom, I just knew how to babysit my nieces and nephews and give them back when they became annoying. I was in my last year at university, which I decided I was going to quit, I lived at home with my mom, and I had just spent £7000 on my car. That could have been spent on my unborn child. What was I going to do?

I was home already and didn't even realise the journey back, my head was in a daze and little Gemini had not interrupted. I said goodbye to Tanya and went inside, marching straight into bed, still fully clothed. I reached for my special notepad that I kept at the side of my bed and started working out how much money I needed to make before I had my baby. I learnt that I was a 'mathematical analysis' type of person, I made a habit of writing figures down in order to process what finances I needed and how I spent my money. I also started writing down the pros and cons of quitting university, when I received a call from an unknown number. I wasn't in the mood to answer the phone, but there was only one person that called me off an unknown number and that was Jay.

I answered the phone, excited to tell Jay my news.

It was Mr. Potter, why was he calling me?

"Hey Seph, it's only a quick call. I noticed that you left class today and we had some important things to discuss, I am your dissertation mentor so I will send you a list of the things that I need you to send to me by next week and then we can get cracking on your final piece," he said.

"Oh…ok." I could sense that this was going to be a tedious conversation. I had no words for Mr. Potter. I was not going to tell him that I was never coming back.

"Is something wrong Seph?" He asked, he must have heard it in my voice and now I was feeling prevailed to give my account.

"Sir I'm…" I paused, not knowing if I should tell him the news I just received. I couldn't.

"Sir, I'm quitting university!" I said confidently.

"You're what?" Mr. Potter sounded surprised. He started to giggle, I think he believed it was some sort of prank. I stayed silent and was getting ready to hang the phone up after feeling embarrassed about my decision to tell him.

I knew I had worked hard for the past two years and I finally started believing that I would be a really good social worker but I was certain that I did not fit into this world. The professional people were not about to take someone like me seriously. I didn't even own a decent suit. All my clothes were high street, my hair was quirky and I couldn't look smart if I tried. I belonged in the ghetto, where I could comfortably go to the corner shop in my pyjamas, I could have bad hair days and no one would frown upon me, I could just be myself and be comfortable. Why was I wasting my time studying? I wish that I could have said all that to Mr. Potter but instead I was just thinking about it in my head.

"Sephuine, I think you need to come into university so that we can talk about your decision, I can help you with whatever you need help with." Mr. Potter sounded like he genuinely wanted to help me but I didn't want the help, the work was not hard, it was what would be expected of me after the course that was hard, the life I was supposed to live was the life that I was fearing.

"Ok sir, I will come in tomorrow." I hung up the phone whilst contemplating if I was even going in. I tried forgetting about the conversation with Mr. Potter and started holding my stomach.

A life was growing inside of me, it suddenly clicked, Jay was on my mind before I got the call from Mr. Potter, I had to tell him he would be expecting a new godchild. Over the years I became very close to Jay, he was my soulmate of the clique and I could tell him anything. He helped fill the empty spot that I felt when my brother went away.

Jay already knew that I had been feeling sick the past few weeks but he would never have guessed it was pregnancy. Jay hated when I spoke to him about sex and intimacy because he saw me as a little sister but I knew I had to tell him that I was going to become a mother. After speaking to him for three hours on the phone he pulled up outside my house. We went through mixed emotions throughout the conversation, some parts getting quite heated but I understood that he was just being a big brother to me and wanted me to finish university and pursue my dreams before getting side-tracked with a child.

I was feeling tired again and it was only 8: 35pm. I said goodbye to Jay and went inside to lie down. Mom had come home and even though earlier in the day I wanted her to stay home, after thinking about my pregnancy, I couldn't bear to face her. I tried staying away from her, I acted busy as if I had mountains of coursework to do so that she could stay out of my room. I had a feeling that if my mom came around me she would have some super sense and just know that her unborn grandchild was present. Luckily for me, my sickness had passed as it usually went away in the evenings and I had retired for the night.

I rushed out of bed to the toilet after having a weird feeling in my belly. Sick again, it was bright yellow and felt as though it came straight from the bottom of my gut. There was so much and I had not even eaten anything. I couldn't believe it was morning already. I woke up feeling angered, frustrated and still very tired.

"You have been sleeping for ages Seph, you didn't even eat dinner yesterday, it was left on the side, are you ok?" Mom was on the landing waiting outside the bathroom door. All I could think about is if she heard me being sick.

"Yes Mom, I am fine, think I have food poisoning Mom." I stayed in the bathroom speaking to her through the locked door so that I wouldn't have to face her.

"Seph, you're pregnant!" She muttered as she walked down the stairs getting ready to leave the house to go to work. How the hell did she know? I hid all the papers that I had off the nurse and there was no other evidence. I unlocked the bathroom door and tried looking like normal Seph.

"Mom you are funny, why would you say that?" I asked her.

"I just know you are, you should have a test done so that you know." Mom said. This was freaking me out, I know that Tanya or Jay wouldn't have told her and my partner would have been too scared to say it without me there. Something was strange, "I messed up and she's found the papers I bet", I said to myself thinking of all the ways that she would know.

"Mom, you are crazy." I tried so hard to change the tone of the conversation as it was starting to make me feel uncomfortable. Mom came to the bottom of the stairs and looked up at me, I could not hold back. The look in her eyes had told me that she knew and I could not lie to her, things were going so good with us and our relationship had become amazing since I started college.

"Mom I'm pregnant!" I dropped my head in shame even though my inner thoughts were happy.

"I know Seph, I just told you that you were," she said as she smiled.

"Well how did you know?" I wondered.

"Seph, you have been avoiding me for the past week, you have been throwing up every morning and you have been sleeping more than usual." My mom had sensed that I was pregnant before I even found out. It must have been a mom thing, I was just shocked that she reacted in a normal way, she must have been ok with me being pregnant.

"Well, I think you will make an amazing mother and I am going to be here for you every step of the way, but you know you definitely have to find somewhere to live now, seems as though you want to be an adult". My mom started chuckling whilst she was speaking which gave me a sense of relief. Mom was on my side for the pregnancy but how was I supposed to tell her that I would be quitting university so close to the end? I needed time to figure it out. I took my phone off the charger as I laid back down in bed, I had two missed calls on my phone, this time it was from my university number. Of course, it must have been Mr. Potter and now he must think that I was avoiding him.

I decided to just face him and hear him out, I owed him that at the very least after all the extra time he spent helping me with assignments and giving me words of encouragement. I waited for the missed calls to accumulate before I made the move to go in and see him.

When I arrived at uni, I saw Mr. Potter in class teaching my fellow peers, I peeped through the glass window, hoping that he wouldn't recognise me there. He looked directly at me and began making his way to the door. I could see Whitney in lesson looking like she was working really hard and just fitting in to this type of life. I wished that I could see myself in that way but I knew that the hood had my heart, I felt torn, between who I was and who I was trying to become. I could see that Mr. Potter did not want to cause a scene, so he ushered me to my chair and told me to get my books out as if it was a normal day in class. I was so frustrated, it had taken me forty minutes to get to Uni today because I had to pull over three times to throw up and now I was sat in a place that I had decided to quit. I felt like walking out instantly but remembered that I was no longer a school child. I was in a place where opportunities were available to people like me and I had to act 'appropriately' as Mom would say. I sat daydreaming about motherhood and all the beautiful things that I wanted to buy for my baby, this was all that I could think about and the fact that I may become violently sick at any given time.

Finally, the lesson was over and Mr. Potter waited for all the other students to leave before approaching me at the table.

"Sephuine, what is this about you wanting to quit?" He asked, staring into my eyes to get a better sense of understanding.

"Sir, I don't belong here, I come from the hood, I mean I come from a bad area, no one goes to uni. No one really aspires to work in these types of jobs, people chase money through selling drugs, having babies, or robbing. I don't fit in with you people. I have to work so hard just to get standard results, where everyone else in class hardly puts any effort in. They don't understand how I talk, they don't understand my life, so what is the point?" I ranted on and on, showing that I needed someone to talk to, sir did not even look surprised.

"Have you come to university for your classmates?" He asked,

"No!" I answered abruptly.

"Have you come to university for the colleagues that you're going to work with?"

"No!"

"Does the lives of these other people determined how successful you are going to be?" He continued.

"Erm, no." The questions were getting trickier.

"In 10 year's time do you think any of these people will be in your life?" Sir was firing questions at me.

"I hope not" I said.

"Look Sephuine, you have to be selfish but self-less when you are going for your dreams, you have to put yourself first because of the successes that you want and fear nothing. Do not let people stand in the way of achieving something spectacular, do not let people tell you that you are unable to do and be a certain way, do not think that you have to change the person you are to fit into a new world. Create your future Sephuine, if you keep telling yourself that you don't fit into the corporate world, then that's exactly what will happen, you will be a misfit of the corporate world. You need to see yourself as a social worker in your world, worry about people fitting into your world and if they don't fit, someone else will. Find people who understand you and who see the potential in you becoming successful. And when you find them, stick by them! Sephuine you can be anything that you see yourself being. You are not quitting University, over my dead body. You have come too far to look back now." I knew he meant what he was saying. He was so passionate and for a moment I imagined him to be my dad speaking to me, which was kind of weird but I was taking it all in. He was giving me strict orders.

I began crying again, I was really becoming a big softy but I was torn. People in the hood saw me and thought that I felt I was better than them because I was going to uni and driving a nice car and people at uni thought I was too ghetto. I couldn't win!

I kept wiping the tears from my face and hoped that everything would just fall into place. Sir continued to fill me with positive and encouraging messages and made me see why I shouldn't be quitting uni even after telling him that I was going to become a mother. He made me aware that he would be with me every step of the way until I finished...

And that's exactly what he did!

He never let the fact that I was pregnant change anything he said. In fact he told me I had more of a reason to finish uni, because now I had to put my child first and do it for them as opposed to myself. I was scared. Scared that I would fail in the corporate world and scared that I wouldn't be accepted. I had to think about exactly what I wanted to do. My mind was unclear. It was like I was being pulled by both arms to see where I could be stretched the most. The stress was building up. "Just quit Seph, you need to focus on being a mom." The little voice in my head always got the better of me, but no one had my back like she did. She was right. Quitting, was the best option.

Lesson 6:

Fear

What are you scared of?

I believe that fear is the most dangerous and powerful emotion that we have as humans. And the reason why I label it the most dangerous and powerful is because, fear has the ability to completely control the direction that our life is going in. Fear will stop you from achieving your dream, fear will stop you from starting your dream and fear will stop you from becoming the best version of yourself. We have all been in a situation where we have experienced fear and some of us are going through it now. It is stopping you from progressing in life.

FALSE. EVIDENCE. APPEARING. REAL

I am here today to tell you that fear is UNREAL (false evidence appearing real). It is simply a perception, a thought that we have in our heads that frightens us so much so, that we freeze. We pause in life and decide that we will not go any further because of a thought that we just made up in our head, that we believe will become true.

Fear is a product of our imagination and only exists in our minds. Most often, I believe people mistake 'danger' for 'fear' but they are completely different, danger is real. Running across the road whilst the traffic lights are on green with moving traffic is 'dangerous'. Running across the road when the lights are on red because you think the cars may hit you... is 'fear'. The difference between the two, is the thought process. We know that the cars are not supposed to move through a red light but the thought of them moving makes us so fearful that it determines our actions when we cross the road.

I mentioned earlier in this book, the battles I faced during my studying years. I really had my mind set on what I wanted to become, but I let fears get the better of me on many occasions. So much so, that I could no longer picture myself working in the environments that I was studying so hard to work in. It took a lot of positive words and encouragement from my tutor, and friends to keep me going. I do not want you to go through what I did! It was horrible. Fear can lead to real mental health issues such as depression, severe anxiety and low self-esteem when you take it to the level that I had taken it to.

How amazing would it be if you could turn your fears into fortune and success? Well guess what? You can! (I wish I knew this when I was 15).

The feeling of fear will happen to every single one of us. You have to use the fear that flows through your body and turn it into something positive. For example, if you have decided that you want to become a better version of yourself, you want to do better things and start feeling like a better person but you are fearful of what the new you may be like, or you are fearful of what others may think, then you need to use that exact feeling against yourself.

You have to reverse the thought process and say to yourself "well what if I stay as I am? Nothing will change", you have to make that feeling override all the previous emotions of fear that you had and use that as a driving force to becoming a better version of you.

It will not be easy, but it will be possible.

Sometimes we create such a big dramatic build up within ourselves that makes us so scared of becoming the person we are destined to become, telling ourselves stories about the 'what ifs' and it's just not a reality. We need to identify the exact fears that we possess, what is it that's stopping you from controlling your destiny and living your dreams? When you know the exact fears that you hold...CHALLENGE THEM with everything you have got. Attack them, because 9 times out of 10, there is nothing to lose.

You always hear people speaking about overcoming their fears and how beautiful the other side was.

The grass is always greener on the other side of fear. That is a fact.

Some of you, are on the tip or the verge of stepping into the best version of yourself but you are letting fear control your life "Oh, I am not going to do this because of this, or I am waiting to start my business because of this, or I am waiting to fall in love because of this." Stop the excuses and tell yourself that fear is not going to be the remote control of your vehicle.

Overcoming Fear!

There are many different ways of overcoming fear in relation to different things in your life. You could be fearful of public speaking, fearful of spiders or fearful of starting a new career in which case, the way that you overcome those situations, will all differ. However, the generic method I use to move forward from my fears is meditation and the urge to 'just do'.

Meditation is when you think deeply about something, focussing for a period of time whilst channelling thoughts that you want to give energy to. Meditation can be used as a form of relaxation and can allow you to spend time with yourself, which is a vital part of life. It doesn't cost any money to meditate and it is a practice that can be learnt by anyone, so do not be discouraged if you have never meditated before. I can help you to start now.

With millions of thoughts travelling through our minds every day, it can all become a bit busy up there in our heads. Meditation can help to calm that down, it challenges you to silence your thoughts in order to get them going at a steady pace rather than in a hectic manner. I would suggest practising for 3-5 minutes, a few times a day if you have never meditated before or for longer periods if you have, just to get used to it. We are going to start right now, and I am here to guide you using the exact methods I use. Meditation is easy, do not be fooled by the literature that tells you that you must be a 'professional meditator'. There are people who are advanced and people who are beginners. There is no right or wrong to meditation, do not over complicate the process. Whether you are advanced or just beginning, we are going to spend the next few minutes having some 'quiet me time' in order for you to start reaping the benefits of relaxing your mind and body.

Task 4: Silence your thoughts!

Using your phone alarm, or watch, set the timer for 6 minutes from the time you start. You can sit up or even lie down on the floor with your eyes closed (this is how I started). It will take you a few seconds to settle down that's why I have warranted an extra 60 seconds for 'faffing'.

- Pick a particular time in the day which best suits you, when you know that you will not be interrupted.
- Find somewhere comfortable to sit or lie.

Sitting with your back straight allows a better flow of energy but sit or lie as you feel to whatever suits you best.

- When you close your eyes, I want you to have a conversation with yourself in your head and tell your thoughts to 'Stop'. Speak to yourself with a calming tone and say 'Stop', the aim is to try and clear your mind by stopping your thoughts.
- Focus on thinking about your breathing. Listen to how you are breathing and then create a slow, steady pattern, inhaling and exhaling. Take a deep breathe in through your nose, filling your body with cool and fresh, present air. And then breathe out, all of your worries and your frustrations.
- Get yourself in a thoughtless state of mind where the only thing you focus on is the present moment, not the past, nor the future. If you find yourself thinking

about other things, then acknowledge the thought but do not energise it with any emotions. Concentrate on your breathing technique and allow yourself to be relaxed.

- Then, sit in silence, practising your breathing until the alarm clock goes off.

Once that is over, your meditation will be complete. Just like that!

I would recommend that you practice this method every day, a few times a day if you can. Once you get into a comfortable routine of practising meditation every day, it will become easier to focus, in which you can extend the time length that you do it for.

It may be difficult to stay focussed when you are just starting out, which is why I suggest starting in little 3-5 minute spouts.

Funny moment; my first meditation session was a serious one, with advanced meditators. My friend Chantel Sachanna had asked me to come along to the sessions that she was thoroughly enjoying. I was a beginner amongst the best. Anyways, I sat with my legs folded and my palms facing up towards the sky, closed my eyes and listened to the guided meditation that one of the monks led. I was struggling to silence my thoughts, I had actually told myself that I was the only one with my eyes closed and that everyone was watching me, in attempt to prank me. Crazy I know. So, I sat for ages battling with myself saying "Seph, do not open your eyes, do not open your eyes" of course I rebelled. The burning desire to just see if I was being pranked had taken over. I peeped out the corner of my eyes to see, everyone was deep into it. In fact, I was the only one with my eyes open. I quickly shut my eyes again before I got caught. However, I spent the whole meditation giggling and peeping. I was a mess!

Moving on, meditation will help you to overcome your fears, because it silences your expressively active brain.

The other method I use to overcome fears, is the 'just do' approach. The 'just do' approach is an aggressive approach which I created that challenges me to face my fears on the spot using 10 seconds (maximum) to deliver the 'just do' thing. It all boils down to comfort zones. As mentioned previously, success does not happen when you are comfortable, things do not get done when you are comfortable and most certainly changes do not arise when you are comfortable. However, it's usually the 'thing' that makes you feel uncomfortable, which is the exact 'thing' you should be doing. That's where my 'just do' rule applies.

Let's say for instance, I have just started my business and I need to call some clients to sell my products. I pick up the phone to call them but I am trembling so badly with fear, that I hang up. What the 'just do' approach allows you to do here, is; pick up the phone, call the client, hear the phone ring and count to ten. (Giving you the time to find your inner beast.) And then allows you to continue to 'just do' anyway. Because the reality of it is, the worse that can happen is rejection. In which case, you move on to the next customer. Did you die? No! Did your business fail? No! Are there many more clients to approach? Yes.

The grass is always greener on the other side to fear and when you reconcile with the facts behind this statement, then you can start to live your life more fearlessly.

Message: It is ok to experience fear as an emotion. But it is not ok to let fear control your destiny.

Chapter 7:

If You Can See It In Your Head
You Can Hold It In Your Hand

A year later than expected and there I was walking through the large auditorium filled with hundreds of parents all there to see their children graduate. Mom couldn't make it to mine and after being so upset about it I humbled myself because Tanya and Skipper had come to support me and were looking after my beautiful little boy. He was one years old. I was doing it for him, one day he would know that I had made it across that stage because of him. I was feeling sick and was sweating more than usual having found out I was now expecting a little princess but I was not going to hold out another year. I wore a beautiful bodycon peplum skirt that fell just below my knees, with a white and black, spotted blouse. Over that was my black gown and my attractive educational crown (the graduation hat). I looked stunning and scrubbed up really well.

Skipper and Tanya went to sit down as I queued up with my class, ready to go on the stage. I received a message from Skipper just before I got on the stage that read "You can do it Seph." This warmed my heart but made me feel nervous thinking about having to walk across the stage. I also received a call from Cyrus and Ricky, who were now, in the same prison, they were making me laugh, both telling me to make sure that I never fell over when walking across the stage. Ricky had brought Jack, his brother a ticket to my graduation. He told Jack that he had to be there in spirit for him and my brother. I hadn't seen Jack all morning so I wasn't sure if he had shown up or not. I hurried them off the phone before prepping myself to walk on the stage. I took a deep breath and tried to calm down my breathing. "I am grateful! I am worthy! I can do anything that I put my mind to! I am wise! I am smart and I am beautiful." The affirmations started to roll off my tongue. Some of the girls next to me, were looking at me like I was crazy. I wasn't sure if they were working for me, I just kept on repeating them as it distracted me from feeling nervous. My belly was turning with nausea just as the girl in front of me had been called. However, when I heard the man call my name immediately after, I put on a brave face and strutted across that stage in my heels with pride, knowing that two years prior I was going to quit university based on my false belief that I wouldn't fit into society. I was working it! A proud mother and social worker to be.

Mr. Potter had made me realise how important it was to not give up, even more so because I was going to bring a child into the world and with it now being my second child coming, the words he told me started to come back. I had to do it for my children. I still believed I was a misfit, being the only one to act ghetto when collecting my certificate on the day, shouting "Woohoo!" And behaving dramatically until I left the stage. It was the perfect memory and I felt prouder than I did on the day that I collected my GCSE's.

To hold my certificate in my hand and take a picture with my son made me so proud, but for some reason I could not shift the feeling of fear. I feared the corporate world, I feared the feeling of being rejected because of the area that I had come from, I feared the feeling of failing and I feared being humiliated if I didn't make it. As much as I felt that way, I still told myself that I had to do it. My ego got the better of me and I had the drive in me to try it out anyway. I was not going down like a sucker, I was about to live for my dream and start working my way up the social work ladder. IRO here I come.

A few months prior to graduation, I had been sitting at home with my son, saving as much as the statutory maternity pay (month in, month out) that I could in order to secure a mortgage. I sat and pondered on my life and knew that I was certain about wanting change. I needed to have my own space in order to think more and to become a responsible adult. So, I moved out of mom's house in Winson Green and into a beautiful brand-new home just in time for my son's arrival. This made me want to own my own brand-new home so badly.

I was researching the internet daily trying to find ways to make money at home because even though it was only maternity pay, it felt good being paid from a space of comfort. It would mean I could be there for every minute of my son's upbringing. The only issue was, the maternity pay that I was receiving was not enough to survive, there was no way that I could make a living with that money and have the finances to travel the world.

One evening I came across a beautiful confectionery gift online whilst looking for something to buy for Tanya's birthday. It was a Sweet Tree, which resembled an actual real tree but the top was made from delicious sweets. I remember adding it to my shopping basket online and getting ready to check out when I noticed that the price was £64.99. Wow! I know Tanya is my best friend but I was not about to spend £65 on sweets for her so I decided to give it a go myself. I was so intrigued by the gift, it seemed pretty easy to make.

I think I spent about £18 on the contents in which some things I had to buy in packs of bigger quantities than I would need. I made it beautifully, I used a purple plant pot and covered it in gold organza material, tied with a dark purple ribbon. I filled the pot with gold pebbles for added effect and used a thick purple rod with gold glitter as the tree trunk. For the tree, I used Ferrero Rocher chocolates which came wrapped in gold paper then wrapped the whole tree in decorated cellophane adding a huge gold bow for the finishing look. It was beautiful and I was so proud, that I took many pictures and uploaded them on Facebook.

The notifications came flooding in and people began asking me how much I charge for them. "Woah slow your roll people!" I said to myself not thinking about the business side to it. 'It was just a gift'- I was about to write as my generic status so people could stop asking me, when it clicked to me that I must have created something so beautiful that it was buyable.

From my early days, I had been very keen to make money, this was standing out as a new opportunity to me, I was so enthusiastic, maybe too enthusiastic actually. Everything started fitting into place in my head, I started to visualise myself having a factory with people working for me, all designing sweet trees of different sorts. "Seph sell them you fool, you can make extra money." The little voice in my head had made her first appearance for the day and I think she had a sensible way of thinking for a change. I'd be a fool to not create a price for the sweet tree's and start selling them. I refrained from writing anything on Facebook and grabbed my notebook and pen. In there, I started jotting down numbers, figures and calculations, it looked like one big mess but I knew exactly what I was working out. I rang my mom to tell her my new business venture and she encouraged me to go for it.

I decided that it was time to start my own business. And just like that I was self-employed! Yaaaaaay!

"This is easy," I said to my son as I cuddled on the sofa with him giving him his last feed for the night. I spent the night gazing at him, "Son I will make you happy. Son you will not be raised in the environment that I was. Son I will take care of us. I am a strong woman, I am brave, I am successful and we are going to be rich, little man." I smiled rocking him back and forth before taking him upstairs to bed. The positive words that Simone had taught me started to resonate with me inside. I really believed what I was saying, in fact I had no choice, I had to believe it because I was not willing for my son to be brought up in the neighbourhood that I was and especially not with the poor mentality folk that were present in that area when I was younger. I was sure to give this business a go and try to be successful at it because I had more than just myself to think about. The excitement in me began to grow and I got straight on Facebook to share my news with my friends.

"Self-employment feels good – I am embarking on my new business adventure." I wrote as my status, before going to bed for the night.

The next morning, I jumped out of bed at 5am, I was the only one awake in the house. I made myself a cup of green tea with honey and started to prepare myself for the entrepreneurial world.

What had gotten into me? I never even drank tea. But I started to adapt the typical 'work from home' lifestyle which usually depicted someone with a laptop, a mug of tea/coffee and a paper. The only thing missing was my newspaper, I started to look the part and it was only day one.

I had received a phone call from a friend who had told me about a new business model that she had been introduced to. She told me that it was hard to explain and that they were looking for more people like me, stay at home moms that are self-employed. I sat there, after putting the phone down saying "Thank you." I could not believe that these opportunities were being thrown at me in every direction. First the sweet business and now this.

I was feeling pumped up and had rang my mom to get her to come along with me to the meeting later that evening. Mom thought that I sounded absolutely crazy and said that she would not be accompanying me to become a part of a private cult. Of course, I never knew much about where I was going, but I had a gut feeling that this was going to work out for me. So, I rang my other friend Ella to see if she could come with me.

(Meet Ella: Ella was the girlfriend of a childhood friend and we met through our partners but just had an instant connection. She was also a full-time nurse).

Ella was always at work so I was hoping that she would be available. When I rang her to ask if she could come to the meeting, she sounded as excited as me and we both planned to meet for 7.00pm. Yes! I knew I could trust in Ella to support me.

At 6: 15pm I picked Ella up from her house. Ella was like me, we hated being late to places and preferred to live life using a more organised approach. We arrived at the meeting early, 6: 47pm to be precise, both oozing with excitement.

We were ready!

We had our pens and notepads and we were just ready to go. The room was filled with all different types of people eager to learn about how they could make money from home. We were all sat in rows of chairs just like an assembly at school but in a more adult environment. There was free juice and water and even free fruits for us to have whilst we listened to all the information.

There was a lady that stood up to speak to us all, she had been telling us about the business and all the ways that people got paid by being in the business. She told some amazing stories, I was so blown away by the excitement in the stories and a business model that paid you in more than one way. WOW!

I sat taking loads of notes, so much that my hands started to hurt really badly. Then the little voice in my head appeared and told me that this was all too good to be true. I became doubtful, I was so frustrated at myself for making little Gemini take over my thoughts again but then I started to agree with her. What the woman was saying sounded great, however, she was a stranger. 'Maybe she was hired for acting' I started to think.

All these great things she was reciting were just words!

The lady was dressed prim and proper in a beautiful fitted grey suit that I know must have been really expensive. It was a dress with the blazer to match and on the inside had a silk purple lining. She looked rich and even spoke rich, how was I even supposed to relate to somebody like that. All these thoughts started to attack my mind. I looked over at Ella in hope to become distracted by what I was thinking. She was still taking down notes with a smile on her face. Surely, she must have been enjoying what she was hearing.

In the break, Ella and I sat sharing notes about what we had listened to.

"Seph! I can't believe it, this sounds crazy," Ella said.

"I know, how mad is this?" I replied. We were hardly saying anything content worthy, we just kept on repeating ourselves, shocked by the many ways we were told we could make money, without having a job. This was great.

After a while, there was another man introduced to the stage. His name was John. He had on scruffy jeans with an off-white t-shirt and some brown shoes. He looked different to everyone else that had been on the stage talking about the business. For some reason, I was interested to hear what this man was going to speak about. I mean, by first impressions he looked like someone from my area.

He began talking by introducing himself and telling us a bit about his background. This guy was cool. He spoke about the life that he came from and most of the things he was saying I could relate to. He spoke about coming from a family that did not have much and this was just like mine. Every few minutes, Ella would look at me and we would nod in unison, agreeing with what John was saying.

Everything was going great until he mentioned the money that he had earned in the business.

WOW! It got better, this was the type of money that I saw Ricky earning. I never knew people made this much money without selling drugs. I was amazed. "This is too good to be true," I said to Ella.

After two minutes of John speaking on the stage, I was hooked. My hands, painfully burning with a tingling sensation, from all the notes that I tried taking whilst the others were speaking but I couldn't keep up. Literally, every word that John was saying was hitting me in the heart. I was starting to think that only Ella and myself were in the room listening. I looked around at the others, sat with no emotion and felt that I had sucked it from their bodies when I began feeling teary.

This man must have been sent down from the heavens, specifically for me, on that day, at that time. The information that he was giving me about where he had come from, to where he is going and how he felt in the process was just so relatable. It was like talking to myself in the mirror, only I never knew where I was going.

Finally! someone that understands me. The lightbulb moment that you hear grown-ups speaking about, had hit me, I was now 100% certain about self-employment and was no longer concerned about plan B, which was to look for a part time job.

The night was over and me and Ella could not stop speaking about how amazing John was. We patiently waited for him to come off the stage and when he was near, darted over to him before anyone could grab his attention. Just like groupies, we were. Proud groupies at a concert.

"John you were amazing," we both said with so much excitement.

"Thank you! So, are you joining then?" He asked with so much confidence. I loved his style, I knew that it must have been this direct attitude that got him so many sales.

"Well Yes." I said, thinking about working with him and all the millions we were going to make. I didn't even know if I had made the right decision, I just remember being told that if I wasn't sure about an opportunity, just say yes anyway and decide later.

Ella and I spoke about John the whole journey home. We were thriving off each other and all of our new plans about the amazing cars we wanted, wedding dresses and beautiful Louboutin shoes that we were going to buy. Everything was becoming a real vision.

I got home and I couldn't believe how much life seemed to be falling into place. My children were about to have it better than I thought. The meeting had totally wiped out the fact that I may need to go back to work. My mind was made up and I jumped on to the laptop to start my training for the business. "Now I have 2 businesses, I can call myself an entrepreneur." I sang as I twirled around my living room with joy. Feeling very happy and awake, I spent 3 hours completing my training that night with my son latched on to my breast.

Life was amazing! Literally, everything that I imagined self-employment was like, was happening.

"Wake up now Seph, this must be some sort of dream" I told myself. But it wasn't. Everything was really happening. I could see a real vision for making a large amount of money without having to work for Ricky. The 'hood' in me was fading, slowly, but surely.

Lesson 7:

Change Your Mindset

In June 2013, my beautiful baby girl was born. I had spent the past few months working really hard at both my business' and earning the most money that I had ever made from working for anyone before. Life was going great and that's because I believed it was, I had become a totally different woman than I was six months prior, my life was in a different place and so was my mind. I began challenging Gemini, the little voice in my head and found ways to filter out her existence if she said something that I did not want to hear. Everything in my life and about my life was good. I was running two successful business' whilst being a stay at home mom, I had enough money and I was able to save towards a new home. This was ultimately my first big dream.

The change shifted when I decided to change my mindset. Changing your mindset is key to everything, not only success but the relationships you have and will later form, your happiness and just your whole life in general. I cannot express through words the importance of what a 'mindset- shift' can do for your life... For the better.

It is known that the human brain produces 70,000 thoughts per day which averages out to one thought per 1.2 seconds. Everything starts with a single thought, whether good or bad, but we will focus on good because I want for you by the end of this book, to be influenced, touched in your heart and ready to change your life and find your true power. Every single one of you has something unique about you, we all have a purpose and when you find that purpose, that thing that you love, that thing that you are so effortlessly amazing at, then believe me you will influence the masses. What is your super-power?

Now, when you read that question above the first thing that happens is a thought, right? That is the 'normal' thing to do when you're asked a question. So, if you are someone that thinks that you will not be successful (as I did when I was younger) due to many different things, or if you think that a certain type of life is not for you because of how you view yourself, then you need to change your mindset because you are pushing yourself away from your super-power.

Some of the most successful people in life have been through a time of doubt, a time of fear, or a time of failure, where they believed they were never going to be in the position that they are today or as successful as they are. But they had a shift in their mindset which lead them to fulfil that exact purpose and with hard work and dedication have achieved amazing success'.

"If you can see it in your head, you can hold it in your hand."

I named the chapter after this quote because this was one of the quotes that helped me to develop and change my mindset. If you are not doing anything to feed your personal development, to better yourself and your mind then you will be vibrating on a low level of life, with the haters, the negative people, the people that don't want you to do well in life and the people who don't have anything. You have to work on yourself, read more positive books, listen to positive audios and surround yourself with positive people, in order to develop yourself. That is the simplicity of personal development.

I need you to know that it is possible to change your mind, this is not something that you will be taught in school so it is important that you learn this now and keep on feeding this notion.

Most people go through life stressed. Stressed and frustrated about the things they never got to do, dreams they never ever achieve and successes that they never meet. Do not be one of those people!

It is possible to eliminate stresses and start living a better quality of life, all from the way that you think about things. It may mean, that you have to follow a programme or add new things into your life that you have not done before, which may make you feel uncomfortable and out of character but when you do different things in life, it will produce different results.

I had to follow a programme! Whatever works for you, do it. But be honest with yourself, if you do not see a change, then change again until you start seeing results. Results will not come over night, so give it time. You will know when your mindset has changed because your energy will be vibrating on a higher level, you will start meeting people that are similar to you and losing people that you thought would be with you until the end. You will start to attract opportunities into your life and you will start to become a better person.

"Thoughts become things."

I first read that quote in the book 'THE SECRET' by Rhonda Bryne. And when I saw the statement for the first time, it meant nothing to me and I never understood it. However, it stuck in my mind and I kept thinking about it because I thought it was a riddle and I just had to work it out to feel 'normal' again.

Then I remember coming across the statement again, in the book 'Thoughts Become Things'.

For some strange reason, this time it was standing out so much, that I could not see anything else on that page. It was almost as if it was written just for me to see at that specific moment, on that specific day. That is when I truly understood the power of the law of attraction.

I started to realise that, the reason why I thought my business was doing so good, was because I was living the business that I envisioned. I had major belief in myself that I could do well and had actually pictured me doing well.

I started to realise that many situations, good and bad, have surfaced exactly how I thought them to be because I had focussed so much energy into that situation happening. So, it was time for me to start focussing my energy on good things, things that would build me up and create this super human that I was made to be.

The Law of Attraction explains that whatever you think about in your mind, and put energy into, will transpire to the universe (your surroundings) in which you will receive the thoughts that you have been thinking.

For example, growing up I always wanted a convertible car, so badly that I could imagine myself driving it. Every night before I went to sleep it would just come into my mind randomly throughout my teenage years.

My second car was nothing short of the convertible that I imagined myself to be in, the colour, the interior and how it drove. It was exactly as I imagined for all those years. And I know you're thinking, this sounds a little farfetched and maybe even untrue, but that exact mentality is what is blocking your mindset from allowing you to be the best version of yourself that you can be.

It's not about being gullible. But it is, about believing that the impossible is possible. Whatever dreams you have, has come from a thought or a desire and the main thing stopping you from obtaining that dream is also a thought, a thought that for some reason that dream you dream is unachievable by you. But dreams can be a reality, there's a reason why your mind can conceive things that you may feel are out of reach and that's because it is possible for you to do, and have.

The problem with our thought process is that, most of us, tend to think about all the things that we don't want to happen and all the things that we fear happening. So, what does that do? It sends out a message to the universe, to all the connecting energies and people around you that, this is what you actually want, even though it is not at all what you want.

We focus our thoughts on worry, debt, problems, issues, and made up scenarios that are not even our reality until we think about them so much and act accordingly until eventually, it becomes our truth. We start to receive more debt, when we are thinking about debt. We start to be comfortable with our normal lives and not take the leap to fulfil our purpose when we pretend that we are comfortable in the situation that we are in.

The simplicity of it is: if you think mostly negative thoughts day in and day out, you will attract more negative things because the universe thinks this is what you want. This is the beautiful thing about the process of mindset, you don't have to stay in that negative mind frame, you can decide to make the change today and start to change your thoughts. Make it your homework—your daily duty—to think something positive every time you realise you have just had a negative thought. You may find this difficult to begin with but it will become easier and you will start to feel comfortable being in this positive frame of mind.

Your thoughts right now, today, are creating and shaping the future that you will have. Everything I tell you in my present state is factual and from experience that I have encountered in relation to myself, it works. I am just a normal person as you are and have been in many situations. My mind was in a negative place, I thought negative things and I believed that good things did not happen to people from my neighbourhood. I was wrong, and the minute I started to believe that I could do better, I was better and I am better!

Be the controller of your mind and tell yourself that in six months time, you will be someone new, someone that will take you closer to your dreams and make you a better person. Challenge your negative voice and find your inner power.

SOME DAILY TIPS TO SHIFT YOUR MINDSET

1. **Read more motivational books.** You have to believe that books are the food for your mind. You have to keep on top of fuelling your mind before it starves and the only way to do that is to read information from people who have already done that successfully. I set myself a goal of reading 10 pages of a motivational book each day, just 10 pages because I did not like to read. Then before I knew it, a year had passed and I had read 3650 pages of positivity, books that were telling me how great I am and books that were fuelling my mind in helping me to change the person I was. I now love to read.

2. **Gently brush your negative thoughts away.** If it is

not real, then do not give it your energy. This can be very tough but once you master this, you are in the game! I used to think up a scenario in my head that would stem from a small thought and I would then let it affect my emotions…yep you heard correct, I could easily think up something, get really upset and angered by it (which would have a domino effect for the whole day) and then act on it. Even though it was just a thought! Maybe fear, rejection, or worry, whatever it was, I would give it all my energy. I mean, it is inevitable that you will think bad thoughts. Something bad will pop in your head at some point, even the most positive thinkers have bad thoughts, you just have to gently brush that thought away.

3. **Listen to positive audios.** YouTube became my best friend. Every morning before getting showered and brushing my teeth, I put on a positive audio. This was as simple as me going on YouTube and typing in 'motivational videos', then I would just listen to everything that they would say. This helped change me drastically and even changed the way I communicated with people. I would get people saying; "Seph, you are so inspiring, you are so positive, you are so wise," to me. I would then be thinking "Wow!" Must be the 'new me' that has formed because I never used to hear those compliments much. From doing this you will find speakers who you can resonate with, or that you feel speak directly into your heart. My favourite speaker is Les Brown – so you can start with him if you like.

4. **Be still for 10 minutes of the day.** I don't mean meditation as such, I mean find 10 minutes of the day to solely think about your thought process. When you are just starting out 10 minutes can seem like a lifetime, but commit to it. You owe it to yourself to listen to your thoughts. Ask yourself how this new

journey is making you feel. You should be feeling better each time.

5. **Positive affirmations.** Now the easiest way to do this is the way I directed at the start of the book when I got you to do the 'I AM' task.

Positive affirmations are statements and words that help you to overcome your negative thoughts and defeat the self-sabotage that you have been committing. They can help you to shape every aspect of your life because they give you belief and help you to actually visualise what you are affirming. When I was first introduced to this, I gave it a try, looking myself in the mirror saying; "I AM GREAT, I AM AMAZING".

POSITIVE AFFIRMATIONS DID NOT WORK FOR ME!

I struggled so much, I felt silly and it felt useless. But I gave myself credit for trying and tried something else. I started to write down the affirmations and read them out loud, that took it away from the main task for me and it became something I was reading, rather than, something I was saying about myself. I also, voice recorded the affirmations in my phone, so on days where I was struggling I just played the voice recording which was my voice, which made it easier to naturally join in with the sound.

You have to find what works for you and implement that because there is a lot of information out there and not all of it will resonate with you, even if its saying the same thing as something that will. I understood the importance of affirmations because most people I viewed as role models spoke about them and if they were doing that and they're my role models, then surely I had to do that to become somewhat near to the successes they have.

I have given you just 5 daily tips that will help you shift your mindset. Start with one of them and then add the rest in gradually.

Task 5: VISION BOARD

As we are on the topic of 'thoughts become things', I understand that now would be the best time to introduce the tool of all tools which will lead you to mastery.

I cannot express how important it is to have some form of vision board to look at on a daily basis, refer back to when you've completed things and as a key motivator to you every day. A vision board can come in the form of a large poster, a digital image or an audio recording, filled with your desires, goals, wants and dreams.

My very first vision board was made from magazine and newspaper cut outs. Creating a vision board is exciting and really challenges you to think further than the dreams you speak about with your friends and family. It gets you starting the action.

I would like you to use an A3 piece of paper and collect loads of free magazines, go on the internet on google and print off the images of all the beautiful things you desire. Carefully cut out your images and get your pen ready to write your goals out. You can make your vision board as beautiful or as plain as you like as long as it fulfils these requirements;

- It is clear in what you are asking for
- The reason why you want all these things
- Only your desires and dreams, no one else's

Once you have completed your vision board (which may take a few days), you can add to it or create new ones as often as you like. Remember to check your vision board on a daily basis and celebrate all of the things that you have accomplished. This will keep you motivated to continue to achieve all that you have asked for, because you will see your visions becoming a reality.

I have selected a few vision boards from google images, to give you an example of what they can look like.

Now that you have had an idea of what a vision board can look like, I want you to start your own. (Use google if you need more examples). Once it is complete, I want you to sign the declaration below which confirms the date that you completed it. It will also be a guarantee to yourself, that you are not going to stop until you achieve all of your goals.

153

Take a picture with it and upload it to our Facebook. (www.facebook.com/sephTHE)

Let's work together as a team to empower one another.

For the first 50 people who do this, I will personally send you a treat from myself as a thank you and well done for taking the step.

Signature:
Date:

Chapter 8:

Shit Just Got Real

Two years later:

I sat with the tears rolling down my face as my mentor comforted me with words of encouragement. I couldn't keep the tears back; my nose was drooling with snot and my eyes were a burning red. The kids were with their dad for the day and I had a business meeting. My life was slowly slipping through my fingers and I was struggling to pull myself back together. After almost three years of a good run at business, a great life and a change of mindset, I began to slow down…drastically. I was burnt out! I had turned a blind eye to all my problems and became good at bottling things away. When friends and family asked if I was ok, my usual reply would be yes. I always hoped that somebody could see past my false pretence of being ok but no one noticed a thing. Well at least that's what I thought until I came to see my mentor.

We had our general catch up, went through self-assessment tax forms, worked out what I am going to be doing next in business and spoke about my previous events. I was chatting away with as much enthusiasm as I could give, when suddenly, he stopped me.

"Seph, I want to end this meeting now and have a quick discussion with you." He said, in a very worrying tone.

"Is everything ok Robbie?" I asked. I could sense that some bad news was to follow.

"The last six times we have met up you have mentioned that you are feeling depressed, let's talk about that." He put his pen down and took his glasses off his face.

What on earth was he talking about? I knew how I was feeling inside but I was confident that I had not mentioned it to him before.

"Me? Depressed? No way," I tried to make Robbie sound as if he was talking nonsense. He started to sort through our previous meeting notes and began pointing to all the times that I had mentioned my depression. I began feeling uncomfortable with embarrassment. I had not even realised that I was crying out for help; each time I had seen my mentor I had given him an insight to how I was really feeling.

I could feel myself letting go. I was about to explode with tears, right there in the meeting. I broke down, putting my head into my hands to hide my face and was hoping for the world to just eat me up at that point. I had nothing to say. I sat in silence whilst I thought whether I should tell him how I had been feeling. I had not told anyone, not even my partner. I was discretely trying to wipe away the tears as I didn't want to seem like a cry-baby. I was a hard knock – I hadn't had a fight in ages but people like me don't just cry for no reason.

The little voice in my head came back;

"Don't you dare say anything Seph." This time I ignored her. I no longer felt like suffering in silence, I needed to tell someone. My mentor was patiently waiting for me to speak. I looked up at him and began telling him everything. I blew my nose before I began speaking and tried picturing something funny in my head to distract me from thinking about crying.

"Things are not going great, in fact, they're not even going ok, things are terrible." I started my rant. I told him everything, the past 17 events that I had attended, I hadn't sold anything, I lost so much money, I used all my savings to invest in business materials, stock and events, I tried investing in online businesses and lost thousands, I was having trouble paying my bills and I felt like I was putting my family at risk of homelessness, I was in arrears with my rent and had no way of paying it. I couldn't even afford to put Diesel in my car because when I checked my bank account online I was in overdrawn by £3.44 with no overdraft. I couldn't tell my partner because I had also lost some money that he thought I had saved and the money that he was giving me for bills was being used for investing in online businesses.

"My life is a shambles Robbie." I continued to cry my eyes out, feeling sorry for myself. Robbie had given me his tissue out of his pocket and would interrupt every so often with a joke which would make me laugh and cry at the same time. Deep down I was broken. I was hurting so badly inside.

"I AM BROKE!" I had told myself that every day for the last several months. All the bills that I had thought about escaping from, were coming through the letter box and parking tickets were being issued to me left, right and centre. I would sit at home feeling sorry for myself and I was taking it all out on my partner and kids. My relationship was on the rocks and I was losing everything.

For that moment, Robbie made everything better. He advised me to speak to my partner about everything and to seek medical help. "Medical help!" I said in horror. This man must be crazy to think that I would be going to the doctors to tell them that I cry most days, I feel down about myself and that life was just not enjoyable for me. No way! How embarrassing would that have been? I told Robbie that I would do everything he advised me to do, and left the meeting.

As I was walking back to my car, I reminisced on the good times I had in my business and when I first started out being self-employed. The joy I felt working for myself and the perks that came with being my own boss, like working the hours that suited me and still being able to be a full-time mom. I began to smile. I felt like a weight had been lifted from my shoulders when I told Robbie how I was feeling. Suddenly I just felt so much better. I gathered that me talking about my issues made them feel less heavy on me. I contemplated talking to my friends but I always saw myself as the listener. I am the one that they come to speak to, I would listen and give them advice. I couldn't possibly tell that them that I was suffering and sometimes not even living by the things I suggested to them. That would have highlighted my hypocrisy and I wasn't about to go down like that.

Different scenarios were playing in my head and I found myself battling with Gemini; she kept on telling me that I shouldn't tell anyone how I was feeling because it would make me look bad. I believed her, I mean she knew me just as good as I knew myself.

Slowly pushing the key through my front door, I thought over and over again about telling someone my issues. Going to the doctor was out of the question, I had already made my mind up that I was not going down that route. I knew that on the other side of the door, was life! I had to be strong for my children and as much as I felt like crying, I had to act as if I was ok. I got in the house, put my bags down, washed my hands and started to prepare dinner. The kids were still out and were not due back for another two hours. As I was cooking I received a call from Simone, she was asking what I was up to and said that she wanted to come to my house to catch up. This was perfect timing as I needed someone around me to cheer me up.

Roughly half an hour later, Simone arrived. We sat and spoke about all the usual things that we would speak about. Simone was telling me to come to a yoga session with her as I was having difficulty meditating. As much as I was listening to her, I kept on questioning myself; should I say something, should I not? Until I remembered how I felt when I told Robbie. I had to tell her.

I felt sorry for her as I knew she wasn't expecting me to release so much craziness at once, especially after telling her over and over again that I was ok. But she was ready to hear it and she made me feel so comfortable telling her. I offloaded everything but this time it was different to when I told Robbie. Simone was my best friend, she was so similar to me. She told me everything in hood style (ghetto language). She became really emotional because she couldn't believe that I had gone through so much alone. I was just thankful that she was there to hear everything at once. I felt relieved. Simone began filling me with all these positive messages and reminding me of all my strengths. She just had a way of swelling my head when we spoke because I felt ten times better after our conversations. She sat with me and did a meditation session where we spoke about all the things that I wanted to do in life and how I was going to clear my debt and start again.

She held my hands whilst we did some positive affirmations. I am love! I am light! I am strong! I can make it through any storm! I am a divine being! I am worthy! I am happy! I can achieve anything that I please! I am healthy! I am the creator of my destiny and I am rich. I knew that I was broke but she told me to focus on what was to come in the future, whilst being happy in the present. So, I took her advice.

When the meditation was over and Simone left, I went upstairs into my bathroom and stared at myself in the mirror. I finally admitted to myself that I had hit rock bottom. "Am I depressed?" I asked myself, waiting for a reply from me. I never had the answers, I just knew that I was experiencing a feeling that I never wanted to experience again. Something Simone had said was sticking with me. When moaning to her about how badly I never wanted to feel like this anymore, she simply said to me "Seph, tell yourself that you don't want to feel like this anymore, and keep on telling yourself that until you feel better." I tried doing just as she told me. Staring eye to eye with myself, I started reciting the words. After saying it two times over, nothing changed. I couldn't help but think that what Simone was telling me was a myth, it wasn't working. I became angered. I held on to the sink as I felt my legs slowly losing grip and my whole body fell to the floor. I raised my knees as far as they could go until my head was deeply sunk between them. After feeling like things could get no worse, they began to. How was this happening? At that very moment, my kids walked through the door in the joyous mood they were so used to being in. They were calling to me, "Mommy, Mommy?" I had to make a choice right then and I had seconds to decide my outcome. I never wanted the children to ever see me in the broken state that I was in. I also knew that if my partner had seen me, he would have fathomed that something was wrong with me. Suddenly I heard Gemini appear in my head again, this time it was loud "Get up Seph, everything will be ok." Would it be? I questioned my inner voice. I knew that I had to do something. I pushed my feet out until my toes were pressed against the bath. I heard the children running upstairs towards me. I quickly locked the door so that they couldn't burst in, when I heard a thud.

"Mom, why is the door locked?" My son said, as he was yanking the handle up and down trying to get in the bathroom.

"I'm just using the toilet son." I answered, as I tried getting myself together, "I'll be out in a minute."

"Mom, open the door," he began yelling, "I want to see you."

For some reason, today the kids had decided to be forceful, they were not leaving me alone, almost like they knew something was wrong.

"I'm nearly finished babies, one minute." I said whilst getting up. I flushed the chain to make it seem like I really used the toilet. Then went to the sink to wash my face. When I raised my head to look at myself in the mirror again, I started to giggle. I had a really funny expression on my face that made me laugh to myself. That gave me hope that all of me wasn't in the low because from time to time I would do crazy things like that.

I made the decision at that very moment that I was not going to feel like this anymore, it was draining me every day to be sad, crying, angry and most of all BROKE!

Immediately the gangster in me surfaced, "Seph fix up, look sharp." I told myself. I started over with my affirmations, I even made them into a song so that it was more suited to my personality. I grabbed my red lipstick that I could see on the bathroom storage stand and started to write a message on my mirror to myself.

"When you leave this bathroom, you will leave all the emotions you had in here, they will be flushed away and you will never feel them again – no more pain", the message read. I started to physically flush the toilet chain, after speaking aloud all the bad things that I didn't want coming back, the last one being "I will NEVER be broke again". Flushed!

When I got downstairs the kids ran and greeted me with a massive hug, they felt so warm. I held them tight and was holding them for ages, thanking them in my head for how they made me feel. Everything I do, will be for you both, I thought to myself as squeezed them tighter. I wouldn't let them go. They were laughing and shouting "Mommy, let me go." The moment was beautiful. I started to feel blessed and began thanking the universe for everything I had received.

I was so used to being this positive person, a good friend and great listening ears for everyone. I never really gave myself a chance to sit back and reflect on how my life was going and how I was feeling. So, I burnt out. I do not know exactly what triggered my feeling of depression, but I do know that for about a whole year I was faking the way that I was feeling. In my head I was broken, but to everyone else I was still, happy Seph.

It always works out in the end

Simone had asked Tanya, Paris and I if we wanted to go to Gambia with her. At the time, I said no because I had no way of affording it – but I had the urge to go. How was I going to pay for a holiday and have spending money? I sat and pondered on all the ways in which I could go, I knew I had to make the trip. I thought about my bills and the debts I had, then started working out how I was going pay them. After doing all my calculations, there was nothing. No money was left over and there was no extra money coming in. I had no money.

I started spending my days figuring out all the things I used to do when I did have money; how did I make it and what daily things did I do to ensure I had it? Then it all started to come back to me slowly. I spoke with Bridgette, about managing my money and ways in which I could get on the property ladder.

(Meet Bridgette: Bridgette is my 2nd adopted mother who is also Paris' biological mother. She has been a positive role model for me since school when she first taught me of the concept of The Law of Attraction).

Bridgette had told me that she runs a savings group which could help me to save money. The idea sounded great, but I had no money to save. I had to explain my situation to her so that she could understand exactly where I was coming from. She somehow found a way for me that would work in my favour. How did Bridgette always do that? She always had the positive answers to problems I believed were impossible to solve. We worked out an arrangement and she gave me tips on how I could make money accessible to me.

I made it my duty to create opportunities for myself. I knew that I wanted to be self-employed, but I did not have the money to invest in a business. So, I chose to start with investing in myself. Every morning when I would wake up, I would do some positive affirmations, I had to tell myself how amazing I was before I started to forget. "I am beautiful, I am light, I am love, I can do amazing things, I am successful, I am a great mother." The list went on. I would ask myself every day "How do you feel today Seph?" This would ensure that I was reflecting on whatever I was doing and taking the time out to actually think about how I felt. I loaded my phone, my car and my laptop with positive audios of motivational speakers and I started to read more motivational books. I was in transition mode. I knew the woman I wanted to become, she was visible and I just had to start walking to her.

A few days later I came across an opportunity online that helped me to make money from my laptop. So I took the opportunity, completed all the training and learnt the ins and outs of what was required to start, to build my bank account back up. I had a huge belief in myself and since I told a few people about my depression period, it made things so much better. The more I spoke about it, the easier it became to speak about. I would get friends building up my confidence by telling me how great I was. Things were picking up, I got myself a part time job as well as working online and my money began to build up.

I was at home one evening sitting in my kid's room, they were out at their nans house for the weekend and I was writing down all the things I was grateful for. I decided, when I had my breakdown that I would start to write things down when I felt really good so that if I ever experienced a really rough time again (which would be likely), that I had something to reflect back on that reminded me of my happy days. It was just before midnight, when my phone rang; it was my mom. She had called to say that my cousin Shaks was fighting for her life in hospital and may not make it. I felt numb, my stomach started to churn and I found myself struggling to breathe. This couldn't be true! My cousin also suffered from sickle cell, and had come into complications with the disease. I couldn't speak to my mom, she told me as I sat in silence whilst listening to her in a manic state. I came off the phone and spoke with my sister Grace. I didn't even know what to say, but something in me was telling me, it was a false alarm; everything was going to be ok and that they just needed time. Shaks was a fighter, I had spoken to her a few days prior and she did not even tell me she was in hospital. She sounded great when I last spoke with her. A call was coming through from Cyrus that I had to take as I knew he had heard the news. My phone was ringing non-stop as text messages were flowing in from our family group chat and it was all about Shaks. I knew something was wrong, this couldn't be a usual hospital trip. Cyrus had been reassuring me to stay positive and that everything would be ok. I couldn't find the words to speak much because I was scared.

When I came off the phone I sat in silence, I started reading over the things that I was previously writing down and nothing was registering. I lay on my son's bed with my head in the pillow and tried to silence my thoughts. I messaged Shaks in hope to get a response from her, I told myself that she will reply to me when she wakes up. A few hours later, after all the messages and calls, mom had called me back again. I thought it was another update call to tell me exactly how Shaks was doing.

"Seph…" Mom paused as I heard the emotion in her breathing, the words just wouldn't come out.

"No, No, No." I said, as my eyes started to fill with water.

I just knew that something worse was to come. My mom began whaling and saying something, I couldn't make out everything she was saying I could just hear her saying not again. I knew what was to come but a part of me needed to hear it, to accept that what I was thinking was the truth.

Two months prior, my grandad passed away in my mom's arms. I remember getting the call and my mom was screaming as a child would who couldn't find their parent. My grandad had cancer and was sent home at the very last stage as there was nothing more the doctors could do for him. My mom and sister had gone to get him from the hospital and brought him home to rest; we were expecting him to be here for a few more weeks, but as they got him in his house and carried him up the stairs, he took his last breath in their arms. It only felt like yesterday that we had laid him to rest. The family was hit hard and my mom was broken. I pieced together that by Mom saying "Not again!" That she meant another death.

"Shakira has passed away!" She cried, as she told me. My phone hit the ground and my breathing became tight. I broke down, I couldn't even speak at that moment.

My cousin had no more fight left in her. In an instant, she was gone. I bawled like a baby for about 40 mins non-stop. I couldn't believe what had just happened. I called Simone and told her what had happened. She too cried on the phone with me and expressed how sorry she was. Simone had met Shaks previously when she came to visit in the holidays. In fact, Shaks met all the clique. In the summer when she came to visit from America, we all stayed at Skipper's house; well that was the plan. Skipper had invited Jay, Simone, Tanya, Grace and me to his house whilst his mom was at work. We were having such a good evening but we weren't supposed to be there.

Our moms would have killed us if they knew we were staying out at a guy's house – our parents never understood until we were older, the friendship all the clique had. So, we were all at Skipper's house and then we heard the sound of a key being put in the door. It was his mom. Skipper began telling us to hide and tried making us hide behind the sofa in the living room. He turned all the lights off and then closed us in the room in hope that his mom wouldn't come and find us. Shaks, had realised that we had left all of our snacks on the floor and knew that we needed to dispose of them fast. "Shall I put the cookies in my boots?" She said, as she grabbed her Timberland boots that were in sight. We all laughed before getting caught by Skipper's mom and thrown out his house.

All the memories started flooding back to me, I came off the phone to Simone and cried myself to sleep. My cousin was gone.

Lesson 8:

Live In The Present Moment!

Life is for living and sometimes it takes you losing something, to understand how important it is. You hear older people saying, "Life is too short," yet it's the longest thing we know. You cannot wait to live, wait to be happy or wait to fulfil your dreams. You have to recognise that every moment is precious and the minute it's gone, its gone and there is no getting it back. You have to live good, focus on being a better person and finding happiness in every moment that you can.

A Message to Shakira

> Thank You, for making me open my eyes to living life. You left with no warning and you created an urge in me that is indescribable. It is because of your leaving that I am sharing my message and fulfilling my purpose. My heavenly Angel, walk with me, guide and protect me on this beautiful journey we call life.
>
> I love you. X Rest In Paradise

Chapter 9:

The Only Way Is Up

12 weeks on...

Your Taxi is outside – my text message read. I scurried around the house pulling my last bits and pieces together. "Have you got your passport Seph and your money?" My partner shouted from upstairs. "Yes, I've got it all, come downstairs, I'm going to go now." I said, as I zipped my coat up to leave the house. I gave my partner a kiss and a hug, told him I loved him and was off out the house.

After telling my partner everything about my past year of feeling depressed and unworthy, he decided that the best thing for me to do, was to go and relax in the sun. He was so understanding and felt that I needed the time away to get myself together.

I will see you guys in Gambia – the text message read from Paris, who was already at the airport waiting for us to arrive. I left my house in good time but was waiting for Simone and Sharon as we decided to share the taxi to the airport. Being late was definitely a 'family thing' for Simone and Tanya's family. Not even a plane could stop them showing up late.

Eventually, we arrived at Birmingham airport and Paris was waiting at the check-in desk with her face screwed up. She was tapping on the desk with her finger and did not look happy to see us.

"Hey Paris." I said, to lighten up the mood.

Simone began smiling before also saying hello. Paris didn't even crack a smile.

"It's not funny, I was just about to check myself in. What time do you call this?" Paris seemed to be upset but her mood didn't uphold for long when the jokes started to surface. Any time us girls got together, it would always be a time of smiles and laughter.

Destination Gambia! I couldn't believe that in just under three months, my life had started to rapidly incline. I was feeling better every day and I was so confident that life was going to be amazing. After all, Shaks had taught me that I had to live life, and I had to live it now. I gave the lady at the desk my bag and rushed to the boarding gate as our gate was about to close. Luckily for us, we made it and we were on our way to Gambia.

The whole plane journey there was amazing. Paris and Simone had been making me laugh for the whole duration of the flight. I didn't even think about my down time, life was on the up again.

The plane landed and all the passengers started to clap. When the doors opened, the warm air travelled through the plane, faster than usual. The pilot said it was 37 degrees. I always looked forward to the warm scent of different countries, it was a gentle reminder that it was relaxation time and that I'd be stocking up on my Vitamin D.

A huge smile crept on my face. It was reflection time for me, I knew I had to completely find myself again. I didn't want to think about what I didn't have and the debt I had accumulated; I wanted to free my mind from any stress and worry and I just felt better.

Banjul airport was nothing like I had ever seen. The residents were so friendly and helpful...or at least that's what I thought until I was told they expected to be tipped for their service. How naïve was I to think that being treated like royalty was a standard requirement? I soon learnt my lesson.

The taxi squeezed all of us in, with our luggage being stringed in the half open boot and drove us to our hotel. When we arrived at the hotel, we were looked after so well (with less tip expectation). It was like luxury; the hotel was on a beautiful beach that served fresh fruit and fruit juices and was loaded with beautiful restaurants.

We headed to our rooms, unpacked our things, freshened up and went for dinner. The people in Gambia were so nice, I had never been to a country before where the residents and workers treated visitors in that way. They had an optimistic way of thinking about life and were so happy. They were positive, regardless of their situation and everyone was friendly with one another. It was like a dream land, with no trouble, no police sirens, no drama and just pure love; very different to the hood.

I was only there for a week so needed to make the most out of this lifestyle as I possibly could. After having a beautiful evening, we retired for the night. Paris, Simone and I were sharing a very basic room, it had three single beds with small gaps in between them, a bathroom and a dressing table. It was clean and done the job. The beach front compensated for the room as we spent a lot of time just soaking up the sun. Paris had a book donation project going on. She had written a children's book on sickle cell called My Friend Jen and decided to donate some books to the children of Gambia.

I spent the whole week meeting amazing people and reflecting on the way that my life flipped upside down in a matter of moments but through it all I found peace. Every day spent in Gambia changed my life even more. I was grateful, I was happy and I was laughing until my belly hurt on most days. I felt blessed to have experienced a place that filled me with so much love. Tanya flew out to Gambia to join us and we had a blast, touring the country, meeting new people and really living as true Gambians would. My time there was going so fast and the only thing I was missing was my partner and beautiful kids.

Very quickly, it was time for me to go back home. I got back to Birmingham to my family and sat all night with them on the sofa just telling them all about Gambia. It was even clearer to me that I had no business staying in the dark place had be trapped in. How did I even get there? I had to climb my way back up. Some days were harder than others but I had experienced a time that I never wanted to re-visit, so my only option was to do my best to never return to that place again. I had to take responsibility for everything that was going wrong in my life in order to fix the problems I was facing.

After all the failures in my business, the two close family deaths, a relationship breakdown, accumulating debt, being angry every day and being broke, I LOOKED UP!

Lesson 9:

Never Give Up

The final lesson is all about never giving up. It is as simple as it reads. No matter how hard it gets, each day that you are blessed with life, take it as a new opportunity and a new chance to start or continuing building your dreams. We all have encountered some crazy things in life; some of us have had a really bad struggle, where as some of us, would have had life a bit easier. We may have faced a re-occurrence of pain, drama and losses that we just cannot seem to fathom; things that we question, that we ourselves cannot find the answer to. Despite all of this, there is ALWAYS a way to turn

When something bad is happening, things are going wrong and you start to feel depressed or down, it is easy to think that these feelings will last forever. They won't.

Every single one of us have an inner strength, you have it and I have it. We have a super-natural power as human beings that most of us do not unlock because we become so content and accepting of the way life is, even if we are not where we want to be. It is only when you experience a situation where you have to give more of yourself than you knew you had, that you are able to unlock the power which you have. That inner strength is present in us all and that survival instinct is just waiting to be fuelled. You just have to believe in yourself.

Find the joy in knowing that when you have hit rock bottom, the only way is up! How cool is that? That the only direction you can go when you're at the bottom is up, that alone should bring you joy and fuel you to turn your struggle into something beautiful. You are amazing and no matter what struggle you go through, your amazingness can never be taken away from you.

Throughout the book I briefly touch on significant situations that have been turning points for me in my life. We all go through them, but I decided to turn all of my situations into positive lessons that have helped me to become a better person. If I did it, you can too. I was just a normal girl, that didn't have much, I grew up in a rough area, but I had a choice and I chose a different lifestyle. It wasn't hard, I made the decision and stuck with it and that's exactly what you can do. If you can relate to my journey and have even experienced more pain, more struggle and more hardship than this, then use your story to empower people because trust me, there is someone out there that is going through the same thing and needs someone to reach out to them to show them that it is possible to bridge the gap and become better. You don't have to stay in the position you are in now, you need to set yourself free.

A lot of people that I conversate with in my profession, are having a hard time with life because they focus on what other people think about them. If you focus on what people think about you, you will never strive to be the best you can be, because their perceptions of you will start to become your reality. Forget about what others are thinking of you. If you have judgemental or negative people around you, then you need to get rid of them; they are toxic. If you feel you are someone that spends a lot of time thinking about what others think, then you need to build your self-confidence.

Self-confidence in my opinion is; having the ability and belief to know that you can do anything you put your mind to, even when all the odds are against you. Having self-confidence can take you a long way in life and I am living proof of that. I have lived my whole life around self-confidence, putting myself in situations where I am no longer nervous about the outcome of things because I have rehearsed and practiced the end result and what is required of me 1000 times over. I put myself in a 'I am so good at this' state of mind and it becomes exactly that. An example of this is my job interviews. I have a 100% pass rate with job interviews, meaning, every job I have been interviewed for, I have got. That then left me with deciding whether I wanted to take the job or not. Self-confidence is a skill and to build mine up, I have used three simple daily tools and rules which are now so intertwind in my routine that I no longer view them as chores, but as habit.

1.   Belief
2.   Repetition
3.   Reward

You will have learnt from lesson three in the book, the importance of believing in yourself so I will not go into that now, but, I will say that believing in yourself is the key ingredient to building your self-confidence.

The second thing I stated was repetition. Repetition, practice and persistence can help to build your self-confidence. What is the best way to become better at something? To practice it and to repeat it, right?

When you keep on doing something over and over again even when being rejected, even when failing, even when being told NO, it is by the law of nature that you will become better at it. Your mind starts to change, you start to become comfortable in knowing exactly what you are doing and you start to believe that, no matter what, you can do it. Famous singers, football players and boxers, all do years of practicing before we see them presented to us, and that's because they are presented to us when they are confident and ready. They have practiced enough to be granted the professional title within their field, which would have taken hard work and a lot of self-belief.

Have certainty in knowing that you can handle what life has to throw at you because you have rehearsed the reaction over and over again. This will build the confidence you have within yourself.

The final tool I use is; reward. This step is huge, you must reward your process of change in order to recognise that you are doing something. Praise your positive behaviour, remember to reward yourself with small treats. I always buy myself something nice, maybe a bag, some shoes or a book. Something that rewards me for completing that very thing, I set out to do.

Are you working on your dreams? Are you taking all the steps you need, to ensure that you reach your goals? Are you doing a little bit of something every day to prepare yourself for success? Are you doing things that you don't normally do, in order to have things you don't normally have? Are you comfortable?

Most of us are living in our comfort zones, and what I mean by that, is, we are living and doing the things we are used to doing but expecting some sort of miraculous change. A change will not come from your comfort zone, I can almost guarantee you that. You have to do things that make you feel uncomfortable, maybe it's making an extra phone call that will benefit your business, or starting to do your daily affirmations in the mirror, meditating, speaking in front of an audience or having to ask someone for an opportunity. Whatever it may be, you have to take the leap because staying comfortable is going to make you stay exactly where you are.

You are the captain of your ship, you decide exactly how far you go in life and you must take responsibilities for failures as well as achievements. Stop beating yourself up about you and feeding yourself with all the reasons why you cannot do better and start to fill yourself up with the good stuff. Keep a journal – start to build a life port-folio of values, growth and life experiences. Then you can reflect on your growth, your goals and the evolution of your life.

Start today

Message: Never stop trying. Never stop believing. Never give up.

Chapter 10:

Finding Your Why

Ok, so now that you have learnt the fundamentals to changing your mindset, you should feel more equipped to start your new journey to finding the better you. However, you will need a reason why you want to become a better person. Something to stimulate you and drive you to keep on going, no matter the circumstances. That is your 'Why'.

What is that one thing that is going to keep you going, no matter what?

The answer to that, is your purpose! When you discover what your purpose is you will start to fulfil the action needed to get you in a state of living for your purpose.

Your purpose is that thing that you love to do, so effortlessly and your 'why' is the reason you have to do it. Maybe it's a skill you have, a talent or a passion for helping others. Whatever it may be, find it! And if you have difficulty finding your purpose as I did, then start with your why. Why do you want to become successful, have a great life and lots of money? The answer cannot be 'because I want to'. There has to be something more substantial that lies beneath the reason why you want success.

My why is my two children. I wanted to create a life for them that I could only dream of, I wanted better education options for them, better financial savings for them and I wanted to get them assets so that they wouldn't have to struggle the way I did just to make ends meet. That is enough for me to get up every day, even on days where I don't want to, to ensure that they have a great life.

Final message: If you want to change your life, you first have to change the way that you think!